Storage, data, and information systems

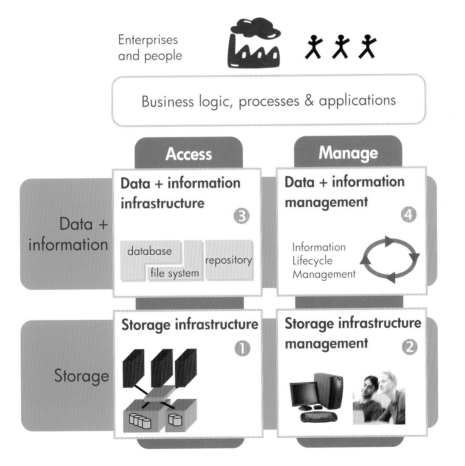

Storage, data, and information systems

John Wilkes
Christopher Hoover
Beth Keer
Pankaj Mehra
Alistair Veitch

Hewlett-Packard Laboratories, Palo Alto, CA

Storage, data, and information systems

by John Wilkes, Christopher Hoover, Beth Keer, Pankaj Mehra, and Alistair Veitch.

Published by: Hewlett-Packard Laboratories, 1501 Page Mill Road, Palo Alto, CA 94304. © Copyright 2006, 2007, 2008 Hewlett-Packard Development Company, L.P.

The information contained herein is subject to change without notice. The only warranties for HP products and services are set forth in the express warranty statements accompanying such products and services. Nothing herein should be construed as constituting an additional warranty. HP shall not be liable for technical or editorial errors or omissions contained herein. If you do find errors, or have suggestions for how the contents could be improved, please send them to storage-data-book@groups.hp.com.

Publication history:
>   5th edition: v5.0 January 2008
>   4th edition: v4.0 January 2007, v4.1 June 2007, v4.2 July 2007
>   3rd edition: December 2006

ISBN-13:   978-1-1424-31731-8
ISBN-10:   1-4243-1731-2

HP publication number: 4AA0–2466ENW

Printed in the USA.

Contents

Enterprises and people

Business logic, processes & applications

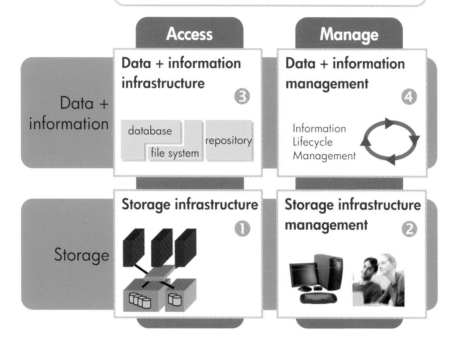

Access

Data + information infrastructure ③

database | repository
file system

Manage

Data + information management ④

Information Lifecycle Management

Data + information

Storage infrastructure ①

Storage infrastructure management ②

Storage

1 Introduction

This book provides an introduction to the technology of storage and information systems.

As researchers and technology experts in this field, we are often called upon to describe the areas in which we work, talk about the trends, and explain why people using these technologies make the choices they do. We ourselves find the questions – and the answers – fascinating, but others tell us that the fog of acronyms and insider jargon makes the technology difficult to understand, disguises the constantly-changing nature of the tradeoffs, and confounds its users.

Our goal in writing this book is to make the technology more accessible and the decisions that people make around it more understandable. We have tried to provide straightforward (but not simplistic) explanations of often-complex technology, and to explain many of the commonly-used terms and acronyms.

To accomplish these tasks, we divided the storage and information landscape into four main sections, each of which is illustrated in the diagram above, and each of which forms a chapter in this book. You will see a small version of this figure repeated in the corner of each page to help you navigate through the book.

The remaining chapters are as follows:

Storage infrastructure discusses the hardware and software underpinnings for everything else. It describes disk drives, how they function, and how they are aggregated together into more complex storage hardware such as disk arrays. We also cover how storage is connected to computers, as well as descriptions of techniques used to store data reliably in the face of failures.

Storage infrastructure management highlights the challenges a system administrator faces when trying to manage a large, and often heterogeneous, storage infrastructure and its sophisticated software components. These challenges include making sure data is backed up appropriately, protected from hardware errors, secured against malicious use, and stored for as long as needed. We describe how these tasks are changing through the increased use of virtualization (logical grouping of resources) and automation.

Data/information infrastructure describes the software and hardware used to store and organize application data, and the three most important ways in which that data is structured: file systems, databases, and repositories. We also introduce the important concept of metadata, or information about data, such as when it was created and who owns it. Obtaining, creating, and exploiting such metadata helps make the data itself more useful.

Data/information management addresses the emerging challenges and opportunities in managing data in our increasingly information-dependent lives. Specifically, we describe the concept of Information Lifecycle Management (ILM), which is a way to structure how information is treated from creation to archive or deletion. ILM seeks to tie the business value of information to the mechanisms and policies used to look after and store it.

A final **summary** provides some key takeaways from each chapter.

Although the divisions between these areas provide a useful first cut for describing the space, they are not hard and fast. For example, we increasingly see a blurring of the division between the management of the storage infrastructure and the management of the information placed into it.

Massive amounts of digital information are with us today, and more is being collected – at an ever-increasing rate. But this, and the technology we describe, is not the end goal: what matters is how we make use of information and the technology around it to make better, more-informed decisions that improve our businesses and our lives. We hope this book makes a small contribution towards furthering such outcomes.

This book would not have been possible without a great deal of help and support, across many years, from our colleagues and collaborators. We thank them all.

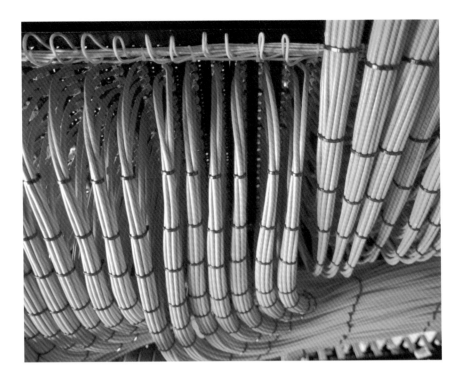

2 Storage infrastructure

In computer systems, *storage* is a container for *data* – the results and working values that are to be remembered. The term *memory* is used to mean storage that is accessed in small units (e.g., a single 32-bit word, or a 256-bit cache line); the term *storage* is usually reserved for memories that are accessed in larger units such as a 512 byte or 4 Kbyte block.

Storage devices usually hold several orders of magnitude more data than memory devices. They also take much longer to access. Most memory is volatile, meaning that it loses its contents when turned off; most storage is non-volatile, meaning that it doesn't. (A familiar counter-example is flash memory, which is increasingly being used in consumer devices such as cameras because it is non-volatile.)

We will be talking about storage here, not memory.

By convention, the letter "B" stands for bytes and "b" for bits. Disk drive space is measured in powers of 10 (e.g., $1GB = 10^9B = 1\ 000\ 000\ 000$ bytes), computer memory sizes in powers of 2 (e.g., $1MiB = 2^{20}$ bytes $= 1\ 048\ 576$ bytes). The international standard for this is to use "Mi" rather than "M", although this notation is not yet in widespread use.

2.1 Disk storage devices

The most important low-level recording technology used in storage devices today – and for the foreseeable future – is *magnetic recording*, which relies on the way certain materials become permanently magnetized when subjected to a magnetic field. It is this permanence that makes magnetic storage non-volatile.

The most important computer storage device today is the magnetic disk drive – sometimes called a hard disk, or a hard drive, or even hard disk drive (HDD). It uses a stack of one or more thin aluminum or glass *platters* (disks) coated with a ferromagnetic film. The platters are spun at high speed – 4 500 to 15 000 revolutions per minute (rpm) – and each surface on each platter has its own dedicated magnetic recording head. An *arm* positions the head over one of the concentric circular *tracks* in the medium, which is where recording takes place; a servo system keeps it there in the face of small deviations and external disturbances.

Electronics in the disk drive amplify and decode the weak signals picked up from the heads, apply error correction to the results (a great deal of redundancy, and special encodings, are used to make this possible), buffer the resulting data, and communicate it to a host computer system on demand.

Disk platters spin at high speed: 4 500 to 15 000 revolutions per minute.

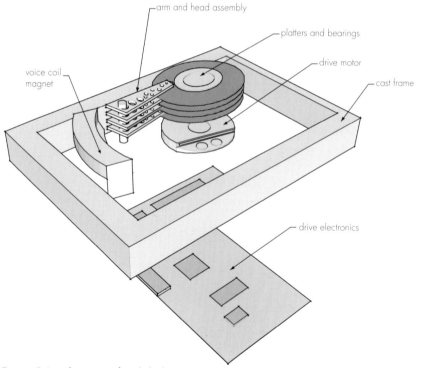

Figure 2.1: schematic of a disk drive

2.1.1 Disk drive types

Disk drives come in a number of different types, and the disk drive market is correspondingly segmented into four general categories:

Type	Speed	Size and capacity	Uses
Desktop	4 500–7 200 RPM 9.5ms seek 70 IOs/s	3.5" up to 750GB	PCs, digital video recorders (DVRs such as Tivo and ReplayTV), and bulk, low-cost storage
Enterprise	10 000–15 000 RPM 3.5–4.5ms seek up to 300 IOs/s	2.5", 3.5" up to 320GB	Mission-critical servers, severe performance demands, and high duty cycles
Mobile	4 500–7 200 RPM	1.8", 2.5" up to 200GB	Laptops
Consumer electronics	4 500 RPM	0.85–1.8" up to 60GB	Mostly portable media players (e.g., iPods), but also phones, cameras, PDA's, GPS receivers

The amount of disk storage capacity being shipped is staggering – almost 30 Exabytes (30 million million million bytes, 30×10^{18} bytes) in 2005. And the rate is accelerating, thanks to the continuing ability of disk drive manufacturers to pack more bits per square inch of magnetic recording medium.

The amount of disk storage capacity being shipped is staggering – almost 30 Exabytes (30 million million million bytes) in 2005.

Petabytes shipped

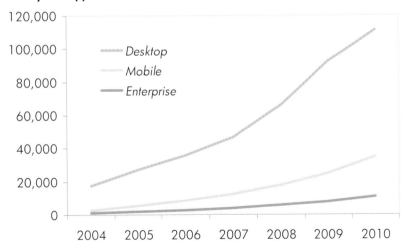

Figure 2.2: worldwide disk drive capacity shipped by disk type. 1 Petabyte = 1 thousand million million bytes, or 10^{15} bytes
(source: IDC, Worldwide hard disk drive 2006–2010 forecast and analysis: record-breaking years may lie ahead, May 2006, IDC report #201478)

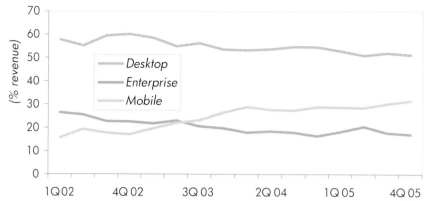

Figure 2.3: worldwide disk drive revenue by disk type
(source: IDC, Worldwide hard disk drive 2006–2010 forecast and analysis: record-breaking years may lie ahead, May 2006, IDC report #201478)

Scaling up a disk drive

Modern disk drives are miracles of precise, cost-efficient engineering and manufacturing. If the distance between the disk head and the platter it flies over were scaled up from its real size (5-20 nm) to 1 mm, then:

- the area of a single 2.5" disk platter would be the same as New York's Central Park,

- the surface of the entire park would be flat to within 0.5 mm,

- the park would be spinning under the head at about 300 mph at its outer edge,

- the arm holding the head would be moving it back and forth at up to 800 mph, and

- the head would be positioned to an accuracy of about an inch, anywhere across the park's surface.

And all for a couple of hundred dollars!

Current disk drives achieve an *areal density* of about 100 Gbits per square inch, but the next generation of recording technology (perpendicular recording, which aligns the magnetic domains at right angles to the platter surface, rather than along it) is predicted to achieve up to 1 Tbit/inch^2 (1000 Gbit/inch^2). This increase in areal density has continued for years, and shows little sign of slowing down soon, despite occasional fears of hitting theoretical materials-based limits (Figure 2.4).

The commodity, cut-throat nature of the disk-drive business means that customers, storage-system vendors, and integrators all benefit from the 30–50% per annum per gigabyte cost-reduction curve.

Enterprise disk drives are less price sensitive than desktop ones, thanks to longer procurement cycles, tighter specifications and lower shipment volumes. In addition, price-per-GB is less important than *access density* (accesses per second per GB) for many enterprise applications. This is what pushes enterprise disk drives to be smaller and faster than the relatively slower, high-capacity desktop ones.

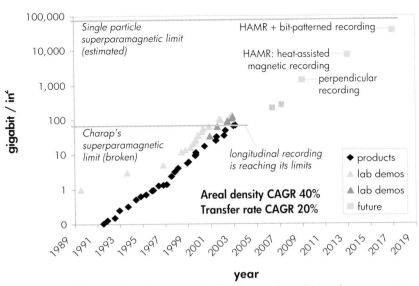

Figure 2.4: disk recording-density trends; the diamonds and triangles represent particular disk drive products; CAGR is compound annual growth rate (graphic courtesy of Dave Aune, Erik Riedel, and Bob Thibadeau, Seagate, 2006)

2.1.2 Disk drive performance characteristics

A vital characteristic of disk storage is that it is a *random access* medium, i.e., the sectors (blocks) on a disk can be read in any order. However, it still takes time to move from one sector to another. That *positioning* or *access time* has two components: the time it takes to move the disk arm to get the head to the right track (called *seek time*), and the time it takes for the data to rotate until it us under the head (called *rotational latency*).

A smaller platter size means less time to move the heads to the right track (i.e., smaller *seek time*), and higher spin speeds, which in turn increases the data-transfer rate and reduces the time for data to come under the heads (i.e., less *rotational latency*). It also keeps the power requirements under control: spindle-motor power grows with the 4.6th power of the platter diameter, and the 2.8th power of the rotation speed – i.e., doubling the diameter increases the power by a factor of 24, and doubling the rotation speed increases it by a factor of 7.

If the next sector to be accessed is adjacent to the last one accessed (i.e., on the same track, and the next one to come under the head), then there is no positioning time. As a result, such *sequential* accesses are considerably faster than *random* accesses – ones that send the head across the surface. For example, a modern enterprise disk drive can retrieve only 200 blocks per second if each one involves repositioning the head, but about 100 000 blocks per second if the accesses are to sequential blocks.

Much of the complexity of storage software (in disk arrays, operating systems, file systems, and databases) is driven by this "access gap" in performance: it makes sense to do almost *anything* to avoid having to go to disk.

Sequential accesses are considerably faster than random accesses.

Scaling up a disk access

If we scaled up the times to access memory and storage to a human timescale from their real values (250ps : 1ns : 100ns : 5ms for a processor to access register : cache : memory : disk respectively), then:

- Looking up something on the paper in front of you (up to a few seconds) is like reading from the processor's cache memory.

- Retrieving a book from the same room (1 minute) is like getting to main memory.

- Seeking out a block of data from a disk is like having an entire bookcase delivered to you – after a wait of 35 days!

- Once the first bookcase had been delivered, more could then come in at the rate of about 300 bookcases per day, but only if they had been stacked right next to each other at the storage depot (library), and as long as you had somewhere to put them.

- You could ask several different libraries to send you a bookcase – but each could only handle one request at a time, and they would probably all have different, unrelated sets of books in those bookcases.

2.1.3 Disk-to-host interfaces

Disks are only useful if they can receive data from, and deliver data to, computer systems. This is achieved by means of their *interfaces*, which connect the disk to the outside world. There are many different kinds of interfaces, but all can be classified according to four main properties:

1. The **physical connection medium** – copper wire or optical fibre.

2. The **type of physical connection** used:
   - parallel SCSI) (Small Computer Systems Interconnect) – a bundle of wires with a wide, flat connector;
   - IDE or pATA (parallel ATA) cable – the flat ribbon cable used inside PCs;
   - SATA (Serial ATA) and SAS (Serial-Attach SCSI) – both use the same 4-wire cable, as replacement for multi-wire ribbon cables or bundles;
   - FibreChannel – an optical fibre connection (copper-wire versions exist, but aren't used outside storage system cabinets);
   - USB (Universal Serial Bus) and FireWire)/IEEE 1394 – "plug-and-play" external connections; for storage, an external drive enclosure is used to hold an ATA or SATA disk drive and provide the conversion to these connection types.

3. The **command protocol** or language spoken across the wires – how operations like read and write are expressed:
   - SCSI (confusingly, the name is used to describe both a connector, a protocol, and a command set);
   - ATA (a somewhat simpler command set, used initially in disk drives for personal computers, from whence its name – the IBM PC/AT-Attachment).

4. The **network protocol** used to encapsulate commands on the wire:

    - iSCSI encapsulates SCSI commands into the packets of internet protocols such as TCP/IP, which enables it to run over any internet-protocol-capable link, including Ethernet;

    - all the others use connection-type-specific formats (e.g., the FibreChannel Protocol (FCP) is roughly FibreChannel's native equivalent of iSCSI).

For a combination of historical and market-driven reasons, high-performance (and higher-cost) disk drives tend to speak the SCSI protocol, while lower-performance, lower-cost disk drives typically speak the ATA protocol. Other properties tend to be tied to the choice of drive-protocol: SCSI disks tend to have higher reliability, for example, and use more expensive components to achieve this.

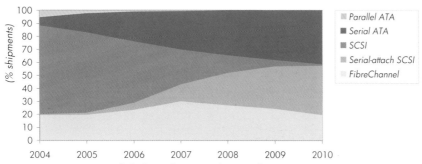

Figure 2.5: enterprise disk drive shipments by interface type
(source: IDC, Worldwide hard disk drive 2006–2010 forecast and analysis: record-breaking years may lie ahead, May 2006, IDC report #201478)

As the graph above illustrates, the more modern serial-attach standards (SATA and Serial-attached SCSI, or SAS) are becoming dominant, thanks to their higher communication speeds and ease of use, lower costs, and greater reliability. FibreChannel retains a relatively constant 20% of the high-end market, where transitions take longer because of the large investments required to change legacy product lines and customer perceptions and because of the installed base.

One trend not shown here is the use of Internet-based protocols to talk to storage devices: we will discuss this in the section on storage networking (section 2.3).

2.2 Tolerating failures

Disk drives break. Networks and wires lose connections. Computers stop working. Users make mistakes. Viruses corrupt and delete data. Software has bugs. All are threats that storage systems are expected to handle.

This section discusses disk array data-protection techniques; chapter 3 (on *Storage infrastructure management*) discusses how broader protections are provided.

2.2.1 RAID – Redundant Arrays of Independent Disks

Availability is the likelihood that a computer system is going to be up when you need it. It is usually defined as the fraction of the time that the system is not down. Downtime can come from failures or planned outages; and is usually approximated

SCSI drives tend to have higher reliability, and use more expensive components to achieve this.

by the product of the failure rate or outage rate and the time it takes to bring the system back up, once the downtime starts.[1] This means that availability can be improved by decreasing the failure rate, or decreasing the time it takes to put the system back together after a failure, or both.

Unfortunately, for data storage, it's not enough just to be able to get to the system that stores the data – the data must not have been lost in the meantime. How well a storage system does this is measured by *reliability*, which is the probability that data will have been retained since it was stored. The most commonly used measure for reliability estimates for storage systems is the Mean Time to Data Loss (MTTDL)) – or, more usefully, its inverse, the annual rate of data-loss events.[2]

Failure rates

Disk drive reliability is usually quoted in terms of *Mean Time Between Failures (MTBF)*, or sometimes *Mean Time To Failure (MTTF)*. A typical quoted value for a disk drive is 500 000 hours, or about 60 years. This is highly misleading: what is being described is an average failure *rate* across a large population of disks, not the expected lifetime of a single disk drive, which is probably closer to 3–5 years of active use.

"What does MTBF have to do with lifetime? Nothing at all! It is not at all unusual for things to have MTBFs which significantly exceed their lifetime as defined by wear out – in fact, you know many such things. A "thirty-something" American (well within his constant failure rate phase) has a failure (death) rate of about 1.1 deaths per 1000 person-years and, therefore, has an MTBF of 900 years [...]. Even the best ones, however, wear out long before that." [3]

Much better is to think in terms of the expected failure rate over some period – and a year gives convenient numbers. A 500 000 hour MTBF equates to an annual failure rate (AFR) of about 1.8%, which also helps remind us that this figure is a mean across a large population, not the actual value that any one disk will see.

Even this is a simplification: it assumes that all failures are independent, and happen at a constant rate. Neither assumption is correct, so it is best to treat the published AFRs or MTBFs as optimistic bounds when doing calculations.

For a system with one disk, the data loss rate just equals the disk failure rate, but for a system with data spread across N disks, the data loss rate is N times worse. For a large-scale computer system with thousands of disks, disk failures can become common events. (A thousand-disk system will experience a disk failure about twice a month). Clearly something needs to be done.

---

[1] availability = (1 – downtime/interval) = (1 – (outage_rate × outage_duration)/interval)

[2] MTTDL is defined with respect to *any* amount of lost data – regardless of its size or importance. This is obviously a crude measure: for a bank, losing one image of one customer's check is far less damaging than losing the entire account balance data for all its customers. Customer psychology, as much as anything else, has precluded rational development of this field's terminology and metrics.

[3] Kevin C. Daly. *MTBF (Mean Time Between Flareups, er, Failures).* In: comp.arch.storage *Frequently-asked questions (FAQ).* June 2004 (accessed May 2006) http://www.faqs.org/faqs/arch-storage/part2/section-151.html.

Once upon a time, high-end IBM mainframe disks could hold large amounts of data, and had outstanding reliability by the standards of the day – today we'd consider them low-capacity, failure-prone, and hideously expensive. With the advent of the PC revolution in the 1980s, disk drive manufacturers started producing small, cheap, somewhat failure-prone disks, and somebody had the bright idea of putting these together to get the same performance and reliability as the high-end drives, but at a fraction of the cost.

Getting the reliability right was the harder part: and the thing that made the difference was encoding the data onto the disks in a way that let the ensemble keep delivering data even if one of the disks failed. This is RAID – a *Redundant Array of Independent Disks*.[1]

The original RAID ideas almost certainly came from a team working on IBM's Series/38 computer system in the early 1980s, but RAID got given its catchy name, and was popularized and systematized, by David Patterson and his students at UC Berkeley in the late 1980s.

The basic idea is simple: spread your data across many disks (to get better performance), and then add some extra "redundant" information to compensate for the drop in reliability that results – in particular, to make it possible to work out what must have been on it if one of the disks fails. The term "redundant" here doesn't mean superfluous or unwanted, but alludes to the idea that the additional information isn't strictly necessary in the no-failure case. However, it's that very redundancy which makes it possible to recover from failures.

The big design tradeoff in RAID systems is between the amount of redundancy (which takes storage and so costs money) and the performance of the resulting system. Inside a disk array, the extra data is typically somewhere between 5% and twice the original data size.[2] Unfortunately, the performance story is less clear – it depends on what you are using the RAID for. And, perhaps most surprisingly, more space devoted to redundant data doesn't always result in increased reliability – it depends on how you use it.

To keep track of the various approaches, the UC Berkeley team gave the different schemes numbers, called *RAID levels*. "Level" is a slightly unfortunate term as the levels have nothing to do with goodness: a bigger-numbered level is not necessarily better than a smaller-numbered one. Nonetheless, this is the terminology that is in widespread use.

RAID *(Redundant Arrays of Independent Disks)* technology has revolutionized the protection of data.

---

[1] RAID originally stood for Redundant Arrays of *Inexpensive* Disks, because the approach was being compared to the Single, Large, Expensive Disks of IBM mainframes, or SLEDs.

[2] To cope with whole-data center failures, not just a single disk, it's easy to get up to 6–8 times as much redundant data as original data. And that doesn't count backups …

The commercially-important RAID levels are as follows:

level	name	summary	design tradeoffs
RAID 0	striping	no redundancy – just spread data across N disks	cheapest, but N times more likely to lose data than a single disk
RAID 1	mirroring	keep multiple complete copies (2 is common; 3 sometimes necessary)	best performance of the fault-tolerant schemes; most expensive storage needs
RAID 10	striped mirrors	RAID 1 + RAID 0 together	same storage cost as mirroring, but better average performance; 1/N the reliability
RAID 5	rotated-parity	for every N+1 disks, devote 1 disk's worth of space to redundant data, and spread it across all the disks	good performance for reads, bad for small writes (e.g., OLTP, online transaction processing). Cheapest data-protection.
RAID 6	multi-parity	like RAID 5, but uses 2 disks' worth of redundancy data in every group of N+2 disks	as for RAID 5, but worse small-write write performance and better failure-tolerance

RAID 0 (striping) has better performance than a single disk, but potentially much worse reliability.

2.2.1.1 RAID 0 – striping

The simplest scheme actually has no redundancy: it just spreads the data evenly across the available disks by placing a portion of data on disk 1, the next portion on disk 2, and so on, going round-robin across all the disk drives. The portion of data put on each disk before moving on is called a *stripe unit* (about the same size as a disk track works well), and each set of stripe units put onto the disks at the same offset is called a *stripe*.

This approach (RAID 0) provides better performance (or access density) than a single disk by allowing multiple disk arms access to the data, but it also reduces the availability and reliability by a factor equal to the number of disks used, which is the motivation to add redundancy.

RAID0: **striping** — no redundancy

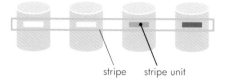

stripe   stripe unit

RAID1: **mirroring** — full redundancy

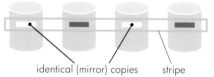

identical (mirror) copies

RAID10: **striped mirroring** — full redundancy

identical (mirror) copies   stripe

Figure 2.6: mirroring and striping

2.2.1.2 RAID 1 and RAID 10 – mirroring and striped mirroring

To get protection against disk failures, the simplest thing to do is to make a second copy of the data – *mirror* it. If one copy disappears because its disk breaks, there's the other one to turn to.

This second copy greatly reduces the chance of losing data, but doesn't completely eliminate it: if the second copy breaks before the first one has been repaired, the data is truly lost. You can improve reliability by keeping more copies (but that gets expensive), or by reducing the repair time (which requires automation).[1]

Mirroring can be combined with striping: first stripe the data across one set of disks, and then mirror these to another set. This is called RAID 10, from the combination of RAID 1 with RAID 0.

2.2.1.3 RAID 5 – parity striping

The cost of complete copies (as in RAID 1) can get prohibitive (or be perceived as prohibitive) for large-scale storage systems. To address this, it's possible to use an *error-correcting code* to append less than a full copy's worth of data while still preserving the ability to recover lost data if some of it vanishes (e.g., if a disk drive breaks).

The *parity* error-correcting schemes divide up the data into stripes (as in RAID 0), and add a single additional block (the *parity block*) to each stripe. The value

---

[1] In a simple 2-disk system, the rate of any data loss is derived from the chance of the second disk failing before the first disk has been replaced:

$$\text{rate\_of\_any\_data\_loss} = \text{failure\_rate}_{disk} \times (\text{failure\_rate}_{disk} \times \text{time\_to\_repair})$$

stored in the parity block is calculated by doing an exclusive-or (XOR) operation on the data blocks in the stripe. This has the useful property that if any single block of a stripe is lost, then its contents can be reconstructed from the XOR of the remaining data and parity from that stripe, simply by XOR-ing the remaining blocks together.

RAID5: **parity-protection** — partial redundancy

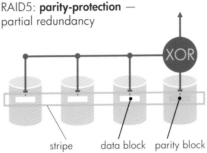

stripe   data block   parity block

Figure 2.7: RAID 5 – parity striping

Unfortunately, the parity block is a hot spot: it has to be recalculated (and rewritten) any time any of the data blocks in its stripe is changed. To prevent this hot spot from always putting load on the same disk, the parity data for each stripe is written to a different disk drive – wrapping around, as before. This is RAID 5.

RAID 5 is so common that the term *RAID* alone is often used as synonym for it. RAID 5 can tolerate the loss of a single disk before permanent data loss; it is quite space-efficient (only 1 extra disk drive for every N); and it has good read performance (almost as good as RAID 0 striping) – but its Achilles heel is the poor performance of writes, because of the need to update the parity.

There's a simple rule of thumb that's good for most applications today: when storage capacity is most important, use RAID 5; when storage performance matters more, use RAID 1 (mirroring).

2.2.1.4 RAID 6 – multi-parity

Stronger error-correcting codes can be used to tolerate more than one disk failure at a time. For example, if two parity blocks are added per stripe, up to two disk failures can be tolerated – this was the first design to be called RAID 6.

Even better protection can be achieved if the additional parity is calculated across multiple, partially-overlapping groups of data blocks, rather than just added independently to each stripe. Many variations are possible; one of the simplest to visualize is a 2D structure, with parity calculated across each stripe, and across all the blocks of data in a column. The SNIA Dictionary now defines RAID 6 as: "Any form of RAID that can continue to execute read and write requests to all of a RAID array's virtual disks in the presence of any two concurrent disk failures. Several methods, including dual check data computations (parity and Reed Solomon), orthogonal dual parity check data and diagonal parity have been used to implement RAID Level 6."[1]

When storage capacity matters most, use RAID 5; when performance matters most, use RAID 1 (mirroring).

---

[1] *A Dictionary of Storage Networking Terminology.* Storage Networking Industry Association (SNIA). http://www.snia.org/education/dictionary/r/, v.2006.2.ENG.

RAID6: **dual-parity-protection**
—partial redundancy

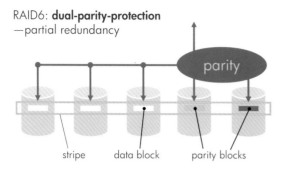

stripe   data block   parity blocks

RAID6: **2D dual-parity-protection**
—partial redundancy

stripe   data block   parity blocks

Figure 2.8: two forms of RAID 6:
double parity in each stripe (top), and 2D parity (bottom)

RAID 6 is becoming more important as the current trend towards ever-larger storage systems continues: single-parity-protection is inadequate for the reliability levels needed at a scale of a few thousand disk drives.

2.2.1.5 Erasure coding

All the failure-tolerant RAID algorithms described above use N data blocks in each stripe, plus one or more parity blocks, and need to read N data or parity disks in order to retrieve or reconstruct the stored data. This works fine when all the disks are in the same disk array, but if the disks are spread out across the network, it generates a lot of network traffic, and can have high latency in a wide-area network (WAN).

Erasure coding is a technique for combining data and additional redundant information to provide failure tolerance against disk loss (erasures) across a set of blocks. Traditional RAID layouts are themselves examples of this, but the term erasure coding is most commonly used to refer to "M of N" encodings, in which *any* M fragments out of a total of N fragments can be used to reconstruct the original data. M and N can be chosen independently: the closer M is to 1, the closer the scheme is to mirroring; the closer M is to N, the closer the scheme is to RAID 5.

One advantage of such erasure coding schemes is that they make it possible to trade network bandwidth for storage space in a distributed storage system. This is particularly important in designs that provide extremely high fault resiliency in wide-area storage systems, which often suffer from unreliable storage nodes (e.g., in peer-to-peer systems), or desire strong availability guarantees in the face of widespread outages.

2.2.2 Reliability calculations and other statistical problems

Most reliability calculations used with disk arrays make many simplifying assumptions – almost all of which are wrong. The common ones are:

- *failures are independent* – i.e., there will be no common factor behind the failures of a group of devices. This is obviously problematic – disk drives are sensitive beasts, so putting them in hot, or humid, or static-prone, or vibrating environments (like an office or factory floor) can significantly increase their failure rate; and a manufacturing-process defect can make an entire batch of drives vulnerable to a common failure mode.

- *only disk drive failures matter* – i.e., ignoring chassis, controller, card, wiring, and other components when calculating failure rates.

- *only hardware failures matter* – unfortunately, not all errors are hardware problems; even though the reliability of storage system software (i.e., firmware) is outstanding, it's getting ever more complicated, and is likely to have defects, however good the testing. Indeed, one of the authors' most painful data losses occurred because of a disk array firmware defect.

- *as long as you have no "single-point-of-failure" you are safe* (a single point of failure is a component or place where a single fault can cause loss of data or access to it) – although this is a good rule of thumb, it's not enough if failure-protection is really important – and sometimes, protecting against the failure of a highly reliable component introduces additional failure modes.

- *failure rates are constant* – the common use of an AFR or MTBF assumes that the rate at which failures happens doesn't change through the lifetime of a component such as a disk drive. It's a convenient approximation, but ignores the larger fault rates often seen at initial burn-in and end-of-life.

All these conspire to make the traditional failure-rate calculations useful only as "guaranteed upper bounds" – i.e., they predict the *best*-case scenarios, not the most likely outcomes. Calculated MTTDL or AFR numbers should be treated with caution: few of them take the factors listed above into consideration.

Failure rates and information about the root causes of failures are usually closely-guarded commercial secrets. Although this makes short-term business sense, it has the unfortunate side-effect of restricting academic research into improvements.

2.2.3 Disk arrays – physical structures

Disk arrays include a few additional components beyond the disks themselves:

- *disk trays* provide power and physical support to the disks themselves, as well as hot-plug support (which is becoming nearly ubiquitous – it allows a disk drive to be pulled out and replaced while the array is in use);

- one or more *disk array controllers*, which run the RAID algorithms and perform management and housekeeping functions; their "front end" talks to the hosts (client computers), their "back end" talks to the disk array's own disks; and

- *cache memory* provides fast access to commonly-requested data, and fast response to host writes.

The simple disk array architecture shown below captures the essence of the idea; in practice, high-end disk arrays are hugely complicated affairs, as the next graphic suggests.

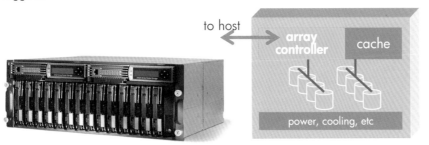

Figure 2.9: a simple disk array (left) and the single-controller version of its architecture (right)

Much of the cost of high-end disk arrays is the effort required to design and build a system that can tolerate every conceivable component failure.

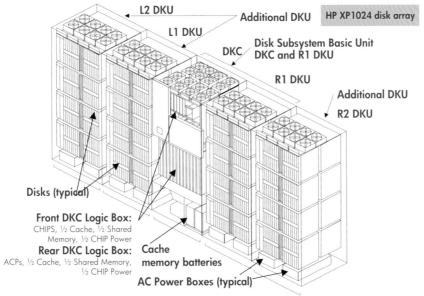

Figure 2.10: a high-end disk array: the HP XP1024 disk array physical structure (a DKU is a cabinet for disk drives; a DKC holds controller electronics)

Much of the cost of high-end disk arrays is the non-recurring engineering effort required to design and build a system that can tolerate every conceivable component failure – including details like shock-absorbing disk mounts, redundant *everything*, compatibility options for connectivity to mainframe systems as well as UNIX and Windows, and huge amounts of testing.

In practice, there are three tiers of disk array in the market:

- *low-end*, with basic features, at low cost (e.g., HP's MSA line). May have single points-of-failure, limited feature sets, or limited performance – at least in some models or configurations.
- *mid-range*, with advanced features, greater range of configuration choices, and proven resiliency in enterprise settings such as SANs, or storage-area networks (e.g., HP's EVA line, EMC's CLARiiON line). Mid-range systems are encroaching from below on the high-end array capabilities, while themselves being pressured by ever more capable low-end systems.
- *high-end*, with all the bells and whistles – and priced accordingly (e.g., HP's XP line, EMC Symmetrix, Hitachi Lightning series). No limits.

Why would anybody pay for the latter? Because they get features that aren't available at the lower tiers, such as mainframe connectivity, more redundancy options (more on this in a moment), very high levels of support, and simplicity of management because each array can do more – although the actual per-box management is probably more complicated than for the lower-tier systems.

2.2.4 Disk array controller functions

Although RAID algorithms help enormously in improving disk-level reliability, and make it possible to build reliable, multi-thousand-disk storage systems, they are not enough. But they do have one big benefit: they provide a place (the disk array controller) where other functions can be provided. Here are the common ones:

- **Caching** keeps a copy of as much as possible of the disk-based data in memory, so that a host gets better performance. Read caching is straightforward, because no harm is done if the cache stops working – the original is still on disk. Write caches serve two purposes:

  1. Improving performance: most storage traffic is very bursty, so write caches make the disk array appear much faster than its disks by absorbing a burst of host writes very quickly, and then writing them out at leisure to the array's back-end disk drives.

  2. Handling some nasty corner cases in the RAID algorithms, such as a power failure half way through a concurrent write to multiple disks.

  Because the resiliency guarantees offered by disk arrays cannot be compromised, write caches are usually implemented with mirrored memories, each of which is backed up with a battery so that it doesn't lose any of its contents in the case of a power failure.

  Battery management is an important chore in disk arrays: the limited time such batteries can support cache-memory state becomes problematic in the case of long-lasting power outages. Batteries are heavy, bulky, and relatively short-lived, which means they need to be replaced all too often – and this has to be done with great care, to avoid accidentally destroying data. The ready availability of cheap, robust, main-memory-speed non-volatile memory would greatly improve these manageability aspects, even if it wouldn't necessarily make the system go any faster or cost any less.

- **Multi-pathing** uses more than one connection point to the disk array, so that it can cope with a fault in the connection between the disk array and its host.

The usual solution is to duplicate the disk array controller, and give each an independent path to the host through the storage network. Both network and controller failures can be handled, with a bit of support from host software.

In turn, additional smarts are needed inside the array controllers: each one has to decide if the other is working properly, or take over from its peer if it has stopped working; they need a way to share state information such as the layout and assignment of data to disks; and they may need a way to access the other's cache memory.

- **Volume management** creates virtual disks (volumes) from portions of data across the array's back-end disk drives. These are called Logical Units (LUs) in the SCSI terminology, and usually referred to incorrectly as LUNs, which are Logical Unit *Numbers*.[1] Volume management includes choosing which disks are to be used for which LUs, which data-protection strategy to use for them, slicing and dicing back-end disks into a few large volumes, or many small ones – or a mixture of the two; and advanced functions such as snapshots and copy-on-write mirrors. Volume management is a type of **block-level virtualization** – described in more detail in section 2.4.

Volumes are virtual disks created by a disk array from its back-end disks.

2.2.5 Disaster tolerance

The discussion above focused on internal-failure tolerance, which is necessary, but not sufficient. What if the entire building that a disk array resides in has to be shut down? One potential approach is *wide-area replication*, across a Wide-Area Network (WAN) such as the Internet, or an enterprise's private data network. In practice, running partial-redundancy algorithms like RAID 5 across a WAN is impractical (too much communication traffic, too long latencies), so approaches here use complete-copy schemes (mirroring).

Some disasters can be handled by having a separate building on the same campus, separated by several hundred meters (500 is a magic threshold for the commonest kind of intra-datacenter optical fibre connection). Then, two disk arrays can be used – each holding a complete copy of the other's data.

Other disaster scenarios require more distant sites – for example, the USA Securities and Exchange Commission is pressing key financial institutions to maintain both a nearby (few km) backup site and a far-away (more than 100km) site, in case of massive regional disruption.

Regulatory pressures

In 1997 the Federal Financial Institutions Examination Council (FFIEC) declared that boards of directors of financial institutions would be held responsible if recovery plans for distributed computing environments are not in place. The FFIEC later expanded this mandate to include enterprise-wide contingency plans in addition to plans for the computing environment.

---

[1] The distinction matters – different array controllers on the same array may sometimes [have to] give the same LU different LUNs. It's a bit like mixing up a person and their name: "I talked to Mark's name yesterday, and ..."

The Sarbanes-Oxley act of 2002 (SOX) makes principal executive and financial officers personally liable for the maintenance of company financial-reporting records – including both business functions and IT assets that contribute to this. Implicit in the rule is that the officers must oversee the company's disclosure controls and procedures and make sure that reports are "timely, accurate and reliable." Although it does not explicitly mandate company-wide business continuity processes, SOX is being interpreted to require either such processes, or an explicit analysis of why they are not needed.

In 2004, the Securities and Exchange Commission (SEC) approved Rule 3510 from the National Association of Securities Dealers (NASD) that required member institutions to create and maintain business continuity plans.

The traditional method of updating mirrored copies requires that the host is only allowed to proceed to its next operation once all copies have been updated. This means that both the local copy and the remote copy have been updated in the disk arrays' caches.

Unfortunately, at these distances, the speed of light becomes a nuisance: it takes about 24ms to send a photon from one USA coast to the other, and 48ms for a round trip (not counting any switch delays) – which is two orders of magnitude longer than the time to access a local disk array's cache. What's to be done? A few techniques have been introduced to handle this problem:

scheme	approach	properties
synchronous mirroring	do nothing special – pay the performance penalty	minimizes exposure to faults, but maximizes network performance demands (to cover the worst-case burst) and the host-visible performance penalty
in-order asynchronous mirroring	try to keep the remote copy up to date, but allow it to get a little behind	in practice, data-loss exposure is small; allows smoothing of network traffic; good host-visible performance; amount of asynchrony can be bounded, at the cost of some performance loss in bursts
out-of-order asynchronous mirroring	as for in-order, but take advantage of the fact that many writes overwrite recently-written data to reduce the network traffic required	better network demands than in-order case, but dangerous if only some of the updates get applied (which can lead to the secondary copy losing its internal consistency, and becoming completely useless); good host-visible performance
batched updates	only update the remote copy periodically	best host performance; most exposure to data loss

This situation is rife with opportunities for mistakes – erroneous algorithms, bad configuration choices, and unforeseen situations can render entire databases unusable if things go wrong. In practice, carefully-managed asynchronous mirroring is probably the best bet for almost all installations, but fear, uncertainty, and good marketing mean that most customers deploy synchronous mirroring more widely than they need, and resort to batched updates when they shouldn't.

2.3 Storage networking

Networks let computers talk to other computers, and modern storage devices are reasonably powerful computers in their own right. The combination of the two can bring the benefits of networking to storage systems, such as sharing storage devices, allowing them to be far away from their clients, and to be duplicated for fault-tolerance.

To understand this acronym-rich space, we need to tease apart the different kinds of features that are involved. Needless to say, there's no neat, orthogonal mapping of concepts to terminology.

- *DAS (Direct-Attached Storage)* is the name used to refer to non-networked storage. Everything else uses some kind of networking.

- *NAS (Network Attached Storage)* refers exclusively – and confusingly – to network-connected storage devices that operate on *files*, not blocks (file servers are discussed further in chapter 4 on data/information infrastructure). All NAS storage operates over the IP (Internet Protocol) stack.

- *SAN (Storage-Area Network)* refers to a network that connects to block-based storage devices; all use the SCSI command protocol.[1] SANs have traditionally been built using FibreChannel physical hardware running the FibreChannel Control Protocol (FCP) as the transport protocol, but this is not required. In particular, a SAN can be built using iSCSI (Internet SCSI), which is based on the Internet's IP-based protocol stack that typically runs over Ethernet.

The following table summarizes the important choices, by asking:

- What is the command set (block or file)?

- What is the physical network (FibreChannel or Ethernet)?

- What is the transport protocol (IP-based or FCP)?

	Ethernet	FibreChannel
command set=blocks	iSCSI SAN	FCP SAN
command set=files	NAS	(empty)

The Storage Networking Industry Association (SNIA) is, as you might expect, active in this area. The term recommended by the SNIA Technical Council (and used in the SNIA Shared Storage Reference Model) is simply *storage network*: a (mostly) dedicated network, used primarily for storage traffic, whatever the protocol it employs.

2.3.1 Storage network components

Most storage networks look just like traditional Ethernet-based networks, whether they are constructed using FibreChannel or Ethernets: they use host-bus adapters (HBAs) in the client computer systems; cables, optical fibres, and switches in the network fabric; and connection points (ports) in the storage devices.

A storage network is a (mostly) dedicated network used primarily for storage traffic, whatever the protocol it employs.

---

[1] The rather confused name "SAN" is presumably meant to be an echo of LAN (Local-Area Network), but what's a "storage area"?

It is still surprisingly difficult to know whether a particular storage system configuration will work, because most FibreChannel protocol implementations are less well tested than their Internet counterparts. Much effort goes into testing a great many different combinations of components, but the task is so daunting that the compatibility matrices that result are often incomplete. For example, a switch might be qualified only at one patch level with a host's adapter card, and only at a different patch level with the disk array the host wishes to use.

2.3.2 FibreChannel

FibreChannel has some unique aspects as a network, driven partly by the desire to minimize cost, and partly resulting from a completely disjoint development path from the IP suites. Two of those unique aspects are *arbitrated loops* and *zones*.

FibreChannel has some unique aspects, driven by the desire to minimize cost, and its disjoint development path from the Internet protocol family.

- **FibreChannel Arbitrated Loops (FC-AL)** are a cost-reduction technology. It is expensive to have to dedicate a full FibreChannel switch port to a single disk drive, so the designers came up with a way of connecting a set of disk drives together in a loop, so that several disks could share a single switch port. This saved money, but added complexity (e.g., the naming process is different from a regular network), reduced failure tolerance, and reduced performance. Use of FC-AL is largely restricted to controlled environments such as inside disk arrays.

- **FibreChannel zones** are a security mechanism: only storage devices in the same zone can talk to one another. *Hard zones* are roughly equivalent to Ethernet VLANs (Virtual LANs) – the isolation is enforced by the switches, and quite secure. *Soft zones* are the equivalent of an unlisted telephone number; when a FibreChannel device asks "who else is out there?" it is only told about the nodes it should be connecting to – but there's nothing to stop it bypassing this list and running amok if it chooses.

2.3.3 iSCSI

The iSCSI (Internet-SCSI) protocols transport the SCSI command set across the Internet Protocol (IP) suite. There are several reasons why iSCSI *will* take over from FibreChannel:

- The sheer volume of the Ethernet business space will drive costs down faster for its widely-deployed technology than for the specialized, lower-volume FibreChannel.

- An IP-based protocol can use existing networking infrastructure, including management tools, cabling mechanisms, diagnosis and repair, etc.

- There are far more system administrators with experience of Ethernet-based networks than FibreChannel-based ones.

- IP-based protocols naturally travel nicely over wide-area networks (WANs), whereas FibreChannel ones have to be packaged up to traverse the WAN.

- At the low end, a client computer doesn't need a specialized FibreChannel interface card, so reducing the cost of storage networking.

iSCSI's use of the Internet's TCP (Transmission Control Protocol) as its transport protocol brings many advantages (including robust handling of packet loss and congestion control), but one disadvantage: because it transfers a stream of bytes, not a stream of blocks, buffer-memory management is somewhat complicated. In particular, it is more complicated than for FibreChannel's equivalent protocol (FCP) – and therefore slower. FCP is implemented by the FibreChannel chip sets, so that host CPU loads are an order of magnitude less than with iSCSI, where TCP is implemented in software.

The current approach to this problem is to develop TCP-offload engines (TOEs) that push some of the TCP processing into the network interface chip, but the general-purpose nature of TCP makes this complicated (and therefore slower and more expensive). Given recent advances in host-side TCP implementations, it is not yet clear which environments TCP offload will be cost-effective for.

As a result, it is still an open question *when* iSCSI will overtake FibreChannel in the market. The shift that was eagerly anticipated a few years ago has yet to take firm hold, but there are signs that it is on the way: Microsoft has started shipping iSCSI device drivers in Windows, for example.

It is still an open question when iSCSI will replace FibreChannel.

2.3.4 Scalable storage infrastructures

With networking comes the ability to have storage devices talk to each other, as well as to their clients. This enables various kinds of scalable storage systems. The "holy grail" here is a storage system design that allows capacity and performance to be added in low-cost increments, and for the total capacity and performance to scale linearly. We're not there yet – but several attempts have come close.

The ideas are not new (a project in this area started at HP Labs in the late 1980s) but the two most recent incarnations we know of are the HP Labs FAB (Federated Array of Bricks) project, and IBM Research's Intelligent Bricks. The latter has the more glamorous hardware story (a cube of storage *bricks* that communicate with their peers in three dimensions); the former has the more impressive software – and software is the real key to success here, not hardware.

These approaches share common themes:

- the use of low-cost, PC-class building blocks (the bricks) that combine processing power with a set of direct-attached disk drives;

- cheap, high-performance networking between the bricks, and from the bricks to the outside world; and

- software that makes it look as if the set of bricks is acting as one storage device: you can send a request to any of them, and they will retrieve or update the data wherever it lies.

Although the individual bricks are reasonably reliable (they use RAID algorithms internally), their disjoint nature means that the ensemble is subject to the problems associated with distributed systems: some bricks may fail or get disconnected; the networks may drop packets; and so on. All these can be addressed with suitable software. Good engineering, and careful attention to detail, result in a system that can indeed provide near-linear scaling across a wide range.

Neither FAB nor IBM's Intelligent Bricks have made it to market yet. But two other distributed storage systems have, each providing a variant of content-addressable storage. One is EMC's Centera, the other HP's RISS (Reference Information Storage

System) (now called the HP Integrated Archive Platform, or IAP). Since both use a higher-level interface than blocks, they will be described in section 4.4 on repositories that begins on page 66.

2.3.4.1 Storage utilities

In the wide area, "The Grid" has long promised the notion of shareable computation and storage for remote users, and several companies came and went during the dot-com boom offering "storage utilities" – storage on tap. Unfortunately, the performance demands of block-based storage access make this hard to achieve across a WAN, so most ended up turning into a kind of co-location business model in shared data centers.

More recently, a few companies (including Amazon) have started to offer a remote-storage on-demand service, leveraging advances in the web services domain, but these have been carefully (and more reasonably) positioned as storage containers for relatively low-performance access needs.

2.3.4.2 Storage on demand

"Storage on demand" is a marketing term used to refer to pre-installing more local storage capacity than a customer initially needs, and then enabling access to it on request. It is used to move part of the ownership risk from the customer to their storage vendor, and so it carries a cost premium. Such storage would have been cheaper if it had been bought up front, or installed along the way. But the premium buys business value: the time to enable access to it is frequently much less than it would take to do an upgrade or install more capacity, and the storage is right there in case it's needed in a hurry.

2.3.5 Wide-area storage networking

IP-based storage protocols can be transported over the Internet directly, usually via tunnels of various kinds to provide security and isolation. But the FibreChannel-based ones have to be encapsulated in an Internet protocol somehow. There are a couple of different ways to do this, but they all need a conversion box at each end.

That box – whether it is providing FCP to TCP connection, or acting as an IP gateway or firewall for the IP-based protocols – represents an opportunity for adding value. In particular, since long-haul networks such as WANs often have limited bandwidth and long round-trip latencies, and much network traffic is surprisingly repetitive, compression and caching can achieve improved performance and lower network costs in the right circumstances.

This is the principle behind "WAN acceleration" appliances, such as the HP StorageWorks Enterprise File Service WAN Accelerator(EFS). Using a proprietary protocol, a pair of these devices (one at each end of a WAN link) only sends each other data that hasn't already been sent across the link. If a chunk of data has already been sent, a short reference to it is sent instead. To users of the link, it appears as if all the network traffic flows as usual, but at a much higher speed for all but the first time through.

WAN-acceleration is most helpful for distant, weakly-connected remote sites, such as small, remote offices (e.g., for an insurance company).

IP-based storage protocols can be transported over the Internet directly.

2.4 Storage virtualization and aggregation

"Storage virtualization" is a catch-all marketing term used for a wide range of topics and technologies that make storage systems better. For example, virtualizing the location of storage capacity makes it possible to just ask for additional disk space without worrying about where those disks reside. The RAID algorithms virtualize the data layout on back-end disks to provide failure tolerance, increased capacity, and better performance. Virtualizing the multiple physical paths between a host and a storage device allows for faster throughput by balancing the traffic load across those paths, and for hiding a path failure by switching over to another one.

Because "storage virtualization" has been applied to so many different things, and many of its uses are simply hype, it helps to ask: *Virtualization of what, and for what purpose?* Here are some example answers to that question:

of what?	to what end?	example
LUs	aggregation: load balancing, performance, scale	RAID algorithms
LUs	volume management: "slicing and dicing"	host-based volume manager, out-of-band storage-management system
LUs	access-control checks	a SAN switch that hides the existence of disk array ports from hosts in the wrong FibreChannel zone
LUs	replication	inter-device (or WAN) mirroring appliance (e.g., HP's ill-fated Continuous Access Storage Appliance, CASA)
network paths	failure-tolerance	host-based algorithms to switch ("fails over") to a new path if one stops working
network paths	increased bandwidth	host-based round-robin routing of storage traffic across multiple paths to the storage system
network paths	security, isolation	encrypting data in flight
LU contents	security, isolation	encrypting data on disk
storage device configuration	simpler management	a management system, console, or appliance

Most of the virtualization technologies are *in-band* – that is, they interpose a component to perform the virtualization in the access path to the underlying entity or function being virtualized. Even the out-of-band virtualization technologies (such as better management) turn out to be in-band when what is being virtualized is made precise.

The SNIA Shared Storage Model is a useful reference document for much of this space. It points out that these virtualization functions can typically be performed in any of three places:

- *host systems*, such as in a logical volume manager, software RAID system, file system, or device driver

"Storage virtualization" is a much-abused marketing term.

- *the storage network*, such as in a storage-fabric host-bus adapter card, a network switch, or a dedicated in-band storage appliance

- *storage subsystems*, such as in a disk array controller

Each place has advantages and disadvantages; there is no one right answer. The choice about which is "best" depends on factors such as:

- how much does performance matter?

- how much does ease of management matter?

- how much does single-solution-type matter?

- how much does cost matter?

- how much does vendor lock-in matter?

- how much do flexibility and scale matter?

- how much does compatibility with other components matter?

Space and time preclude a full analysis of these tradeoffs – but reducing the design space to the axes described above will go a long way toward understanding the technology alternatives.

2.5 Tape and other recording technologies

The discussion above focused on disk-based storage, because that is where the majority of the innovation is occurring, and where the bulk of new data is being stored. Tape storage, however, remains an important component of the storage infrastructure space, and is unlikely to be completely displaced any time soon.

Tape storage is very similar to the familiar audio cassette popular in the 1980's. The magnetic medium: is a ferromagnetic material coated on a thin, flexible ribbon (the tape). *Tape drives* use the same recording technology as disk drives, but move the tape past the heads rather than spin a disk underneath them. Tapes are packaged into removable cartridges, and these have to be loaded into a tape drive before they can be accessed.

One tape drive can access many tape cartridges; since the cost of the tape drive mechanism is typically amortized across many tapes and several years of usage, tape's cost-per-byte is low, although now being rivaled by the cheapest disk drives.

Tape remains an important component of the storage landscape and is unlikely to be completely displaced soon.

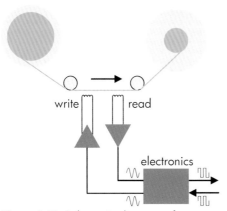

Figure 2.11: Schematic diagram of tape storage

There are many different tape cartridge formats: the most prevalent one today is LTO)) (Linear Tape – Open), which represented 77% of the market in 2004. A current-generation LTO cartridge can hold 400GB of data (twice that with typical compression ratios), and transfer data at 80–160MB/s. It is physically about the size of a 3.5″ disk drive.

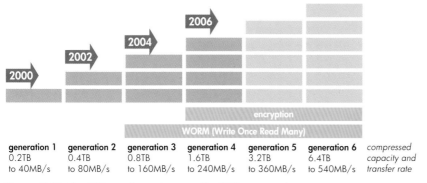

generation 1	generation 2	generation 3	generation 4	generation 5	generation 6	compressed
0.2TB	0.4TB	0.8TB	1.6TB	3.2TB	6.4TB	capacity and
to 40MB/s	to 80MB/s	to 160MB/s	to 240MB/s	to 360MB/s	to 540MB/s	transfer rate

Figure 2.12: the LTO roadmap (source: the LTO program)

Because only one tape can be loaded into a tape drive at a time, tape storage is considered an offline medium, and a person or a robot is required to load a tape and bring it online. Tape drives can be packaged with mechanical movers into *tape libraries*, which can access vast quantities of information, albeit with access times measured in minutes rather than milliseconds.

Tape remains the preferred medium for long-term archiving and offsite backups, primarily because of its removable cartridges, but also because its long-term physical properties are well understood.

2.5.1 Tape software

In contrast to disks, tape storage is a *sequential access* medium. The tape must be read in order, or a huge performance penalty paid. An exact analogy is to VCRs and DVDs – the DVD can skip to the second hour of a video in fractions of a second, while the VCR can take a minute or more to do the same thing. Whereas disk blocks are fixed size, blocks on tape can be of variable length.

Tapes are not usually accessed directly by regular applications; instead, they tend to be used by specialized software that packs files or volume-images onto the tapes. Most such software is used for making *backups* (snapshots of the current state of a system, designed for data-recovery in case of loss) or *archives* (a packaged collection of related data to be kept for future reference).

There are many variations in the way that the backup (or archive) function is delivered, depending on the path taken by the data from where it is stored onto the tape. The *SNIA Shared Storage model – tape addendum* describes these in some detail: the figure below is the overview, showing tape as a parallel access stack to block-based disk storage.

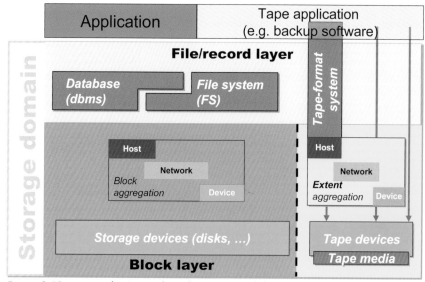

Figure 2.13: tape in the SNIA shared storage model

NVRAM memory has excellent energy efficiency, extreme ruggedness, lower weight, size, and volume.

2.5.2 Virtual tapes

The access characteristics of physical tape drives are somewhat inconvenient: a long wait to load a tape, the need to keep data flowing continuously in order to keep the tape drive operating at full efficiency, and a limited number of concurrent operations that can be performed (one per tape drive).

Virtual tape systems help with this, by presenting the same logical interface as a tape drive to a computer system, but spooling the data at full speed into a disk drive cache, and then writing it to tape in the background. This decouples the performance behavior of the tape drives from the computers that write to them. Preserving the tape interface provides backwards compatibility with existing software.

2.5.3 Non-volatile memory

Most storage is non-volatile, meaning that it doesn't lose its contents when power is removed, while most memory is volatile, meaning that it does. However, some solid-state memory technologies such as FLASH *are* non-volatile; these are often called NVRAM for Non-Volatile Random Access Memory. These kinds of memory are augmenting – and even replacing – magnetic recording technology in some applications.

NVRAM memory has a number of advantages compared to magnetic disk drive technology, including excellent energy efficiency, extreme ruggedness and lower weight, size, and volume for a given capacity. The advantages of NVRAM are overwhelming for some applications, such as portable electronic equipment like mobile telephones, digital still cameras, small personal music players and handheld personal navigation devices. As a result, there is no longer a market for extremely small form factor (1" and less) magnetic disk drives, and the major hard drive manufacturers have discontinued developing and selling such products. In addition, NVRAM is readily available to consumers in cheap, rugged, plug-in modules that give them a convenient way to upgrade their storage capacity and an easy to understand model of "what lives where".

The most commonly used non-volatile memory is called NAND ("not-and") memory after the kind of logic circuits it employs. Before a block of such memory can be written to, the block must first be erased. Erasing is both relatively slow (it takes about 2ms) and slightly stressful, so each block of memory can only be erased so many times (typically 0.3–1 million) before it wears out. These properties mean that special data layouts and file systems are used with flash memory, to even out the wear, and to avoid having to update the same block multiple times in quick succession.

NVRAM memory density and cost trends follow the ones for standard volatile semiconductor memory, such as DRAM, rather than those for magnetic disk drives. At capacities above a few gigabytes, current NVRAM technologies are significantly more expensive than magnetic disk drive technology. For example, a NAND FLASH version of an1.8" or 2.5" magnetic disk drive costs eight to fourteen times more than the disk drive for comparable capacity.

2.5.3.1 Personal computing applications

In concrete terms, replacing the typical 80GB hard disk drive in a laptop with a 64 GB solid-state disk (or SSD) adds about US$1000 to the laptop's retail price. This is justifiable for some individuals, such as a business person who travels and wants the ultimate in portability, reliability, and battery life. But when cost is an issue or high capacity is required, magnetic disk drive technology remains the clear winner. High capacity (> 20GB) personal music players all utilize magnetic disk drives today. This cost differential is likely to persist until at least 2010, preventing the SSD from entering the mainstream as a full-scale replacement for the magnetic disk drive.

2.5.3.2 Enterprise computing applications

When performance requirements trump cost concerns, such as in high-end transaction processing, a non-volatile SSD can be constructed from solid-state RAM backed by a battery and enough NVRAM or hard disk space to write out its contents on a power failure. Such an enterprise-class SSD can handle 50 000 IO/s – well over 150 times the IO/s rate of a single high-end enterprise disk drive – and this directly translates to better application performance. An added benefit is that this performance requires only 1/3 of the power of the high-performance disk

Holographic
recording
remains a future
possibility.

drive it replaces – and power usage is an ever increasing concern in data centers. These advantages don't come cheaply: a high-end SSD can cost nearly $20 000. Until prices come down, such high-end SSD devices will remain niche products.

2.5.3.3 Hybrid applications of NVRAM

Given the disparity in cost and performance between NVRAM and magnetic disk drive technologies, system designers have begun augmenting disk drive systems with NVRAM technology, in an attempt to get the best of both.

Two main approaches are being used. The first, favored by the magnetic disk drive industry and some system integrators, adds NVRAM to the electronics of a standard magnetic disk drive. The NVRAM acts in much the same way as the disk drive's volatile RAM cache does, meaning it holds frequently-referenced blocks of data and returns them quickly to the host, avoiding disk accesses. But unlike the volatile RAM cache, the NVRAM can be exploited safely for writes as well as reads, since it will not lose data if the power fails. This combination offers increased performance and can (under favorable conditions) reduce energy usage, if the disk drive can be powered down when it is not in use. System integration in this scheme is easy: typically the host treats the hybrid drive as a "plain old" disk drive. But the scheme has drawbacks: without deeper integration with the overall system, the performance and energy saving benefits can be lost.

A second hybrid solution that is coming to market places the additional NVRAM under control of the computer's host processor, by wiring it directly to a host bus. This approach is favored by Intel and Microsoft, among others. In this case the host processor, often in conjunction with a special controller chip, actively manages the NVRAM storage, deciding what purpose it should play. The NVRAM may be used to defer writes to a disk drive to avoid spinning it up in order to save energy, as in the first approach. But this is just one of many possibilities. Some of the NVRAM may be used to cache those files read at system startup to accelerate system start up. In one commercially available offering the NVRAM is partitioned to provide both functions.

2.5.4 Other recording technologies

There are other recording technologies. Here is a short list of the most important:

- *optical recording* uses media whose optical properties can be changed by a laser. These changes can be permanent, so optical media are important in applications where data cannot be changed after it has been written, such as for insurance records. In the past, optical media provided higher recording densities than magnetic disks, but this is no longer true. Like tapes, optical media are generally removable, which makes them useful for exchanging data. (Re)writable CDs and DVDs are examples of optical recording media. Because CD-ROMs (read-only CD-format disks) can be mass-produced in a pressing plant, rather than having to be recorded one by one, they are commonly used for distributing software.

- *holographic recording*: remains a future possibility – and has remained so for about the last 30 years. It uses laser holography to record (and read) spot patterns in a 3-dimensional crystal. Information density can be incredibly high

– but the signal-to-noise ratios achieved have not been good enough yet to build a reliable storage medium.

- *MEMS (Micro-Electro-Mechanical Systems)* use thousands of small read/write heads, each of which can write to, or read from, a small area of a medium that is moved beneath them. They offer the promise of high information density, low cost, and rugged operation – but many practical difficulties remain to be worked out.

2.6 Summary

Modern storage systems are built on the foundation of magnetic disk drives – which are both spectacular pieces of engineering, and possessed of access characteristics that much of the storage software stack spends a great deal of effort working around.

Block-based disk arrays provide highly reliable storage, and are the dominant storage components in data centers today. Redundancy is the key to their success.

Storage networking allows storage and its clients to be separated, which in turn allows for storage resources to be pooled for economies of scale and management. Several different storage network types exist, and although the move to IP based storage networks is inevitable, its pace is still a matter of debate.

Finally, magnetic tape remains an important part of the story, although most innovation and growth occurs in the disk domain.

Block-based disk arrays are the dominant storage components in data centers.

3 Storage infrastructure management

Each storage device, each of the connections it has to the outside world, each storage container it provides, and each configuration choice it offers represents something that probably needs managing. *Storage infrastructure management* is the term used to describe that control and management.

Storage infrastructure management appears complicated – because it *is* complicated, thanks to the complexity and heterogeneity of the systems it is called upon to manage, and the diversity of functions it is called upon to perform. One way to clarify things is to divide up the space into orthogonal elements. The following partitioning into three themes is one such division, and the remainder of the chapter is organized around it:

- by **target** (what *thing* is being managed) – e.g., disk array, network switch, logical unit (LU), etc.

- by **infrastructure function** (what *capability* in the infrastructure is being managed) – e.g., data replication, failover, network traffic flow, load balancing, etc.

- by **management function** (what *operation* is being performed by the management system) – e.g., discovery, monitoring, configuring, provisioning, decommissioning, etc.

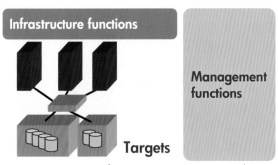

Figure 3.1: storage infrastructure management roles.

A *target* is a
storage-
infrastructure
entity that
needs
management.
Functions
include
discovery,
monitoring, and
control.

3.1 Target-based management

A *target* is a storage-infrastructure entity that needs management. Each storage device, each network device, each network link, and each control or configuration knob they have, generates a need for management.

Before a target can be managed, it has to be *discovered* – which itself is a nightmare in a storage system with thousands of components, and non-trivial even for a small data center. Discovery processes tend to work by scanning their environment – which means that the target must be reachable from the points doing the scanning. Many storage devices have Ethernet ports, and can be managed across the LAN; but many have only their storage-network connections, or are direct-attached. Such devices can only be reached from the nodes that are connected to them – and even this cannot always be done without installing agents onto those nodes (for example, a switch or a host may not be able to report on its local storage systems without first having a monitoring agent installed and activated).

Once the target has been found, and a communication channel established, the usual first step is to start *monitoring* it, to determine if it is healthy (no failures), if it is behaving as expected (no performance or access anomalies), and to generate reports for human consumption. These reports can be used for business processes such as charging for use and capacity management; they can also help with the process of diagnosing problems, either in the storage target or elsewhere in the system. Most existing storage management systems have focused on these aspects, because it was relatively easy to do: much of the heterogeneity between device types can be elided or suppressed by means of abstraction.

The next step beyond monitoring is *control*: effecting changes in the state or configuration of the target. This is much harder, because most storage system targets require very explicit specifications of what is needed from them and impose many, sometimes arcane, constraints on what exactly can be asked of them. To make matters worse, control operations frequently have poorly-defined failure semantics.

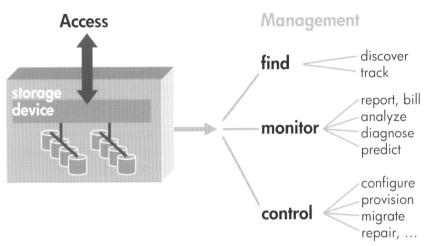

Figure 3.2: target-based management. Several tools exist for the find/monitor functions; fewer for the control ones.

The single most important technology for implementing target-based management is SNIA's SMI.

3.1.1 SNIA's Storage Management Initiative

The single most important recent technology for implementing target-based management is the *SNIA Storage Management Initiative* (SMI, http://www.snia.org/smi). This was created to "develop and standardize interoperable storage management technologies and aggressively promote them to the storage, networking and end user communities." The *SMI-Specification* (SMI-S) defines the functions and interfaces to be supported; version 1.0.2 was approved as an industry standard by ANSI (the American National Standards Institute) in 2005.

The key ideas in SMI-S (Figure 3.3) are:

- management clients and providers (e.g., storage devices) communicate using *models*, written in a format called CIM (Common Information Model)

- the models are emitted by, and consumed by, *providers*, which are access points to target devices

- a common set of core *management services* are defined, and provided by SMI-S-compliant infrastructure platforms (they do things like discovery, notification, model transport)

- storage management *applications* add value on top of the instrumentation layer, by building on both the device state and the instrumentation platform

SMI is a success thanks to some serious cross-industry collaboration, including regular "plug-fests" to test interoperability, and the existence of both marketing and technical teams working to make it adoptable. As a result, the SMI architecture is being widely implemented by storage vendors.

Its inherent flexibility and ability to work with existing monitoring tools means that it is on track to providing a widely-deployed, standardized, information platform on which advanced storage management applications can be written – and it is these that provide the true value to customers. SMI development continues, to cover new storage types, new functions, and better performance. It is also extending its coverage further up the storage stack to include data/information infrastructure components.

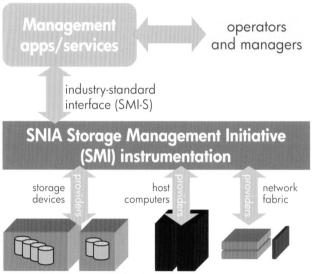

Figure 3.3: overview of the SNIA Storage Management initiative (SMI) architecture

One example of products based on SMI-S is the storage management software produced by AppIQ, now integrated into the HP Storage Essentials suite after HP acquired the company in October 2005. That software offers target-based management (primarily discovery, monitoring and reporting), but it also offers some infrastructure-function control functions as well, such as disk array and path provisioning.

3.1.2 Other target-based management tools

Many network-management players participate in the storage infrastructure management space, usually by extending their existing product base to cover some of the storage management. Since many of them have progressed to target-based management, but little further, we'll enumerate them together here.

- *Network-management suites:* With the increasing use of network-connected storage, network management becomes a key part of storage-infrastructure management. Existing network-management suites (e.g., HP's OpenView, IBM's Tivoli, CA's BrightStor) have been extended to provide additional support for storage devices and the storage networks that connect them.

- *System-management suites:* Datacenter management software suites (e.g., HP's Systems Insight Manager) have long harbored ambitions to take on more of the storage-infrastructure management. To date, the linkages have remained somewhat elusive: "integration" typically occurs primarily at the Graphical User Interface (GUI) layer, where each tool can launch an interface to the other, although a few are beginning to share the configuration management database (CMDB).

- *Remote-support management suites*: A significant remote-support business can increase its productivity by providing remote management capabilities for storage infrastructure, as well as computer systems and applications. Such remote-management suites are largely built around existing management infrastructure, augmented with functions such as automated "phone home" capability. In a few cases, remote support is the vendor-preferred mechanism to effect changes: for example, EMC encourages users of its high-end disk array products to use the EMC remote support facility to make configuration changes – for a price.

- *OS-management suites:* Several operating system vendors and their partners have developed significant storage-management components as part of their system management tools. Almost by necessity, these tools are typically restricted to viewing the storage devices as providers of storage containers, and are rarely able to directly control the storage devices themselves. Nonetheless, they play a significant role in creating virtualized views of storage (e.g., host volume managers); enforcing access controls; and providing load balancing and failure-tolerance.

- *Device-specific management tools*: Every storage-device vendor has to provide a standalone management tool that can connect to the device and configure it, for those installations that have not acquired, or refuse to acquire, the vendor's preferred storage-management suite. The pressures of the marketplace mean that such tools are expected to be "free". These tools have evolved from simple, crude serial-consoles to ones that exploit built-in web servers, and beyond – in some cases, they are limited versions of the more powerful tool sets. The fact that not all storage devices have traditional network connections complicates things: alternate control paths have to be established, such as via a FibreChannel port.

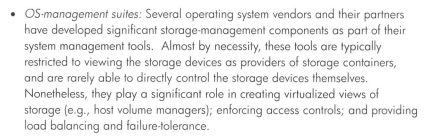

Another way to look at storage management is by the capabilities that are controlled, managed, and enabled.

3.2 Infrastructure-function-based management

The previous section focused on managing the storage devices themselves. Another way to look at storage management is to group things by the features that are controlled, managed, and enabled. There are many such functions: storage infrastructure is called upon to do a great deal more than just storing and retrieving data. Here are a few examples:

1. Keeping a live, active copy of data available in the face of failures and attacks.

2. Keeping multiple copies synchronized (e.g., the on-line transaction processing (OLTP) copy used for order processing, and the point-of-sales data used for forecasting).

3. Moving data around to follow users or changing access patterns (e.g., "follow the sun").

4. Balancing the load across data-access paths, and shaping the traffic across them.

5. Providing support hooks for management operations such as provisioning, data scrubbing, system tuning and optimization, problem resolution, asset

management, Service Level Agreements (SLA) management, etc. These include:

- performance monitoring and reporting
- error/fault detection, isolation, recovery, monitoring, and reporting
- low-level storage device reconfiguration
- active-data migration (i.e., while data is still being accessed)

The first three of these functions all involve data replication, one way or another, and are the subject of the next subsection.

Load balancing and traffic shaping are close in functionality to existing network management, and similar approaches are used. Traffic shaping is not yet commonplace, but will probably become more so as shared storage systems replace disconnected islands of disconnected storage. Such consolidation brings increased management efficiency and higher utilization levels – but also allows loads that used to be disjoint to interfere with one another. Traffic shaping is one way to limit the amount of interference between such workloads.

The range of monitoring and reporting functions that can be provided is obviously large. The current trend is to handle the variety by separating the low-level information-reporting (which can be provided at the storage device level, e.g., by SMI providers) from the higher-level analysis and decision-making. The latter are enabled by the increasing support at the device level for providing device models that can be reasoned about using model-based automation. This allows the complexity of such algorithms to be separated from, and applied across, the details of individual devices. In turn, this makes it possible to provide value-added functions on top of a broad deployment, data-gathering, and management system, such as SMI.

3.2.1 Data protection

Access to trustworthy information is critical to modern businesses, and the regulatory climate is changing to make it mandatory, rather than merely a good idea, to protect data against disasters and other calamities.

As a result, a great deal of storage technology is devoted to improving the availability and reliability of storage in the face of many different failures and difficulties. These cover a huge range, but the most important are probably:

- disk drive failure: the more disk drives, the more likely that one of them will break – and modern storage systems may have thousands of disk drives
- storage system failure (e.g., bad disk array memory, battery, controller board, backplane; environmental problem such as flooding or over-temperature; a firmware defect in the storage system)
- network link failure, or any of the myriad of possible network problems
- configuration problem, such as one that prevents a host from seeing the disk array with its data
- operator error, such as erasing the wrong volume, or connecting the wrong wire to a switch

- user or programmer error, such as writing bad data on top of good

- virus attacks, which can infect stored data

- management system failure, such as a defect in the control system, or the goals or commands it is given

- and a whole range of malicious attacks, such as industrial espionage, government (or hate-group) censorship, and attacks by disgruntled insiders/employees

This list is by no means exhaustive – but it gives some idea of the kind of things that can go wrong, and which storage systems are expected to protect against.

Notice that *knowing* that you are protected (or not) is often almost as important as *being protected* because it allows remedial action to be taken. Technologies for threat assessment and system evaluation are in their infancy, but certainly merit further investment.

3.2.1.1 Metrics for data protection

The key technical measures for whether data is being kept safe are:

- **availability**: what's the likelihood I can get to it *now*? (e.g., when a customer tries to place an order)

- **reliability**: what's the likelihood the storage won't go wrong *over some period*? (e.g., over the legally-mandated retention period for financial data)

Availability measures whether data can be reached; reliability measures whether it is stored correctly.

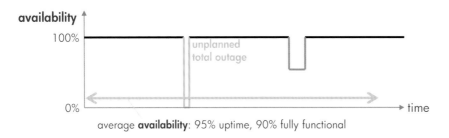

average **availability**: 95% uptime, 90% fully functional

Figure 3.4: availability and reliability

These measures are helpful, but not sufficient. Most data protection schemes take some time to kick in, and may take some time to execute (e.g., to read a backup tape). This means that they take some time to get a system back to an operational state, and may not even be able to retrieve the very latest changes. The effects of these properties can be measured using:

- recovery time: how long does it take to get a system back up and running after a failure? (the *recovery-time objective*, or *RTO*, is the maximum allowed for this)

- recovery point: when you recover, the storage system typically has to go back to an earlier version of the stored data. How far back? (the *recovery-point objective*, or *RPO*, is the maximum allowed for this)

- recovery probability: what's the chance that recovery will be successful? (this aspect is rarely discussed)

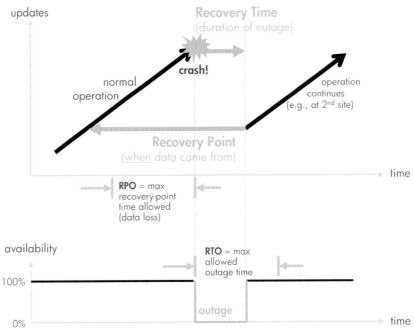

Figure 3.5: recovery time, recovery point, RTO (recovery-time objective), and RPO (recovery-point-objective). The figure shows a system that is processing updates at some rate, and then experiences a failure. The recovery time *is the length of the outage experienced by users of the system; afterwards some of the most recent updates have been lost, as the system had to recover back to a point in its past –* the recovery point. The objective versions of these values (RTO and RPO respectively, shown in blue) specify the maximum allowable recovery time and furthest-back recovery point. In this example, the outage duration is within the bounds, but the recovery point is not – it goes further back than the RPO allows.

Trying to achieving appropriate recovery-point and recovery time objectives is a cause of much management complexity – there are so many different ways of achieving them. But most approaches can be boiled down into one idea: *keep multiple copies of data* – which is also known as *data replication*.

3.2.1.2 Data replication

Data replication touches all aspects of storage, and is applied in many ways. A few are shown here (about as many again didn't fit on the graphic).

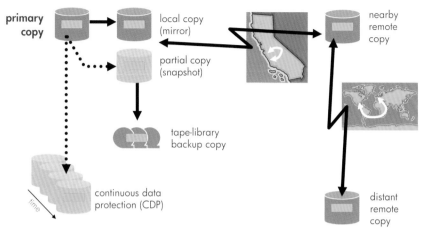

Figure 3.6: some kinds of data replication; the figure is designed to be read starting with the primary copy at the top left; the text below describes the kinds of replicas created

A primary copy of data might be protected by means of:

- a local (mirror) copy, inside the same disk array – protects against disk failure;

- a "nearby" remote copy, in a different data center, but close enough so that speed-of-light is not a major factor in the performance (typically 0.5–50km) – protects against disk array or local site failure;

- a "distant" remote copy, far enough away that the time to update the remote copy is likely to be significant, because of speed-of-light delays – protects against a major regional disaster;

- a copy on tape, e.g., for putting into an archival vault – protects against a errors that corrupt the online copies;

- a local partial copy (e.g., a snapshot) – partly for protection against accidental file deletions, but also to allow the tape copy to be made at leisure, independently of updates to the operational data; and finally,

- (logically) taking a snapshot after every update (called continuous data protection, or CDP) – protects against deletions and accidental overwrites of data by providing "time travel" back to the state of the system in the recent past.

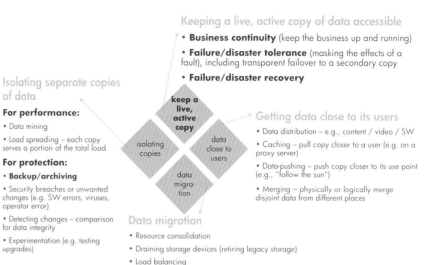

One way to make sense of all this is to examine *why* the different data replication technologies are deployed. The following graphic illustrates the main reasons.

Keeping a live, active copy of data accessible
- **Business continuity** (keep the business up and running)
- **Failure/disaster tolerance** (masking the effects of a fault), including transparent failover to a secondary copy
- **Failure/disaster recovery**

Isolating separate copies of data

For performance:
- Data mining
- Load spreading – each copy serves a portion of the total load

For protection:
- **Backup/archiving**
- Security breaches or unwanted changes (e.g. SW errors, viruses, operator error)
- Detecting changes – comparison for data integrity
- Experimentation (e.g. testing upgrades)

keep a live, active copy

isolating copies

data close to users

data migra-tion

Getting data close to its users
- Data distribution – e.g., content / video / SW
- Caching – pull copy closer to a user (e.g. on a proxy server)
- Data-pushing – push copy closer to its use point (e.g., "follow the sun")
- Merging – physically or logically merge disjoint data from different places

Data migration
- Resource consolidation
- Draining storage devices (retiring legacy storage)
- Load balancing
- Data pushing

Figure 3.7: reasons why data is replicated

One key reason to replicate data is to keep an active copy accessible at all times.

We can divide the data replication technologies into two main schemes: the first keeps multiple, complete copies; the second gets away with only partial copies. For complete-copy schemes, the most important are storage-device technologies such as:

- mirroring (local or remote)

- backup, either to tape or to disk (note that some modern systems are so large that tape-based backup – or, more importantly, recovery – is simply not possible in a reasonable time)

- archiving: to tape, disk, or a repository device

With the partial-copy schemes, the goal is to trade off storage and bandwidth demands against some protection or performance – for example, by only making a copy of data that has recently changed, presuming that a full copy exists somewhere else. The most important partial-copy technologies are:

- *partial-redundancy RAID* (discussed in section 2.2.1 on disk arrays).

- *snapshots*, which record only the differences from some common state. This is usually accomplished by keeping the underlying copy the same, making a map of which blocks have been updated in the new copy, and directing writes to the new copy to a separate place. The result appears to be two complete copies, but they share all but the blocks that have been updated since the split. Because making a snapshot only requires making a new map, rather than copying any data, they can be quite fast to create – a few seconds for a block volume.

- *content-based compression*, in which common sequences of data in input files are identified, and only stored once (see single-instance copies in section

4.4.1). This differs from snapshots in that the latter start out from a known state where the two copies are identical, while this builds up the list of identical fragments from the separate copies.

- *log-based replication*, in which updates are written directly to one copy, but spooled off to the side as well, perhaps with the addition of a copy of whatever was being overwritten. Logging can be done at the block, file, or database level. Operation logging is the special case of putting the requests, rather than the results, into the log; it is commonly used with database systems where a small update can affect many data blocks.

- *continuous data protection (CDP)*, is a form of log-based replication done at the block level. In CDP, it is possible to analyze the contents of the log to present a view of the source volume at *any* prior moment in time that the log covers (sometimes referred to as *"time travel"*).

These each provide some form of tradeoff between the failures protected against and the cost of creating, updating, or storing the copies. All are important in different circumstances. What really matters, however, is not the creation of the copies or redundancy, but its exploitation: *backups aren't important – the ability to recover is.* Recovery techniques include:

- *restore from copy*, which can be kept online or vaulted, local or remote;

- *migrate to copy*: instead of bringing the data back to the processing, move the processing to another copy of the data;

- *time travel:* revert to a chosen point in the past, either a snapshot or a point in the continuous data protection log. This is most used for end-customer single-file retrieval. The term "any point in time" (APIT) is used to capture the idea that you can have very fine-grained control of the moment you go back to.

3.2.1.3 Selecting an appropriate data replication design

Which technology to choose? The list is already long, and new technologies such as CDP and content-based compression are making the choice more difficult, not easier.

One way to handle the alternatives is to assess how useful they are. In particular, when the goal is to keep a live, active copy of data accessible, the choice is [or should be] driven primarily by the *penalty* for failing to achieve this – i.e., how much it hurts if things go wrong. Such a penalty can be measured as the sum of an *outage penalty* or *cost* (e.g., dollars per hour the system is down), plus a *data-loss penalty* or *cost* (e.g., dollars per hour that the recovery point is back in time). If a penalty is measured in terms of dollars per hour, then we refer to it as a *penalty rate*.

Backups aren't important – the ability to recover is.

Figure 3.8: penalty rate versus protection style needed

If we cast the business goals in terms of such penalties, then we just need to minimize the sum of the expected penalties, plus the capital and operating costs of the data protection part of the storage system. This is an optimization problem – something computers are good at.

The graphic below shows the results of one such optimization run: different penalty rates result in different best-technology choices.

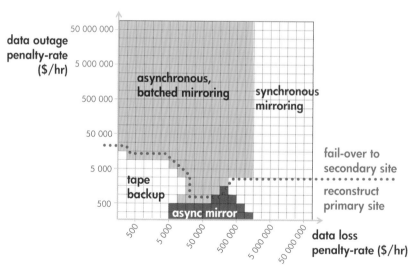

Figure 3.9: automating the selection of data-replication mechanism as a function of outage and data-loss penalty rates (graphic adapted from Designing for disasters, K. Keeton et al, FAST'04, March-April 2004)

Automation is particularly important during failure recovery, when uncertainty, chaos, and pressure are all at a peak: this is not the time for humans to be making ill-judged decisions about the best way to cope. Practice drills can help, but are limited in the range of scenarios they can handle. Automation of these steps can improve both accuracy (and hence recovery likelihood), and also reduce recovery time, by taking advantage of all available resources in a way that a human might not be able to. HP Labs researchers have been at the forefront of work in this space, and UC Berkeley has a major initiative in "recovery-oriented computing".

3.2.2 Data integrity

A particularly insidious problem in large software systems is silent data corruption: data is found to be bad only when it is retrieved, if at all. This can have many causes, including defects in the application generating the data, buffer-management bugs in a database or file system, bad firmware in the storage subsystem, and disk drives that write good data to bad places. Data-integrity techniques can narrow down the likely culprit, and may even be able to prevent the problem, or at least detect it early. Examples of technology here include:

- *read-after-write*: read the data after it is written and compare it against the original (this checks that the data has indeed been written to disk)

- *internal checksums*: compute and store a checksum of the data (a value that is likely to change if the data itself changes), so allow detection of changes in the data between when the checksum was generated and when the data is used (this can catch silent corruption of the data while it is stored)

- *location-dependent checksums*: computing the checksum using both the data and the address in which it should live (this detects data that was written to a different location than it should be in)

To date, most of these technologies are considered too expensive to apply uniformly (especially read-after-write), or are restricted to a few high-end applications (e.g., mission-critical Oracle databases).

3.2.3 Data longevity

Achieving data longevity (which is a mixture of data integrity, reliability and some level of availability) over long periods of time is likely to become more important as society – and commerce – moves more of its assets into a solely-digital form. Consider long-lived content such as multi-decade property leases, and medical records, which have to be held for a few years past an individual's lifespan.

Techniques needed to achieve such longevity are still under development, but they will likely encompass the following:

- wide-area data replication, across multiple organizational and geographical boundaries

- self-checking and self-correcting data formats (including such features as aggressive error-correcting codes, digital signatures and checksums, and processes to check these)

- limits to the rate at which data can be modified (this technique is just starting to be used by some traditional libraries for their digital content)

- techniques such as checking ("scrubbing") the data at appropriate intervals to determine if something has gone wrong, rather than waiting to discover this after it is too late

Achieving data integrity across decades is likely to grow in importance.

- continuous, rolling migrations of data to new storage technologies (which the tape people have been doing for decades)

- storage of application software and an execution environment for it – as well as the data – so that the data can be decoded and understood (how many files written on a 1980s word processor can be read today? Even assuming access to a working 8" floppy drive.)

Long-term data retention is still relatively ill-researched by comparison to short-term, active storage, but will grow in importance over the next decade or so, as regulatory requirements drive retention policies to be more strongly enforced, and as digital media become the primary choice for more and more of humanity's data.

3.2.4 Data security

As with data protection, data security against a wide variety of threats is increasingly recognized as an important issue. Much of the recent awareness is being driven by regulatory changes, which are themselves demanding that businesses protect their data.

The storage infrastructure can help make data more secure in a number of ways:

- ensuring that only authorized entities (people, computers, programs) can retrieve or modify data (e.g., LUN masking, which only allows certain hosts to read block volumes, in-band virtualization of back-end systems that hides inaccessible storage servers, file system and database access controls);

- encrypting data "in flight" to and from the storage subsystem, as it traverses the storage networks;

- encrypting data that is stored in the storage subsystem (e.g., some mobile drives now require a key to be provided at startup); and

- automating (or hiding) complex operations, to reduce the risk of mistakes.

Access controls do certainly help, but they are probably best at helping to avoid accidental mistakes, and should not be relied upon to preclude serious attacks, given the sometimes convoluted settings that must all be aligned correctly to get the right mixture of security and ease of use.

Encrypting data, especially if this is done at the source, rather than solely in the storage system, can help considerably, but the management of the keys (passwords) used to encrypt data poses significant challenges – generating them, distributing them, ensuring that they are never lost (or can be recovered if necessary – and only if necessary), and re-encrypting material when a key has been compromised.

Encryption and other security schemes only help if they allow an organization to continue to get done what it needs to. Specifying the goals and policies associated with security remains a thorny area; in the future, expect to see greater tie-in between security-policy systems and storage systems management – e.g., the use of role-based controls to define the scope and capabilities of (storage) system administrators.

3.3 Management-operation-based management

So far, this section has discussed the management of storage targets and storage infrastructure functions. To tie these together with the overall business objectives, it is necessary to consider management processes and functions that are driven by IT objectives and processes, rather than by the underlying technology, components, or capabilities.

To illustrate how all the previous aspects come together, we will consider one example: that of provisioning a new block volume on a host system, in order to support a new file system or database. The scenario is illustrated by the graphic below, which also shows some of the components that need to be configured to add the new volume – from the physical disk array at the bottom, through the storage network fabric, up to the host itself. Working bottom-up, the new volume needs the following done before it can be used:

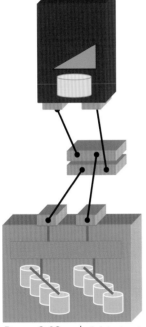

Host computer:
- file system
- logical volume manager
- storage-network interface cards

Storage network switches:
- storage network switches (zones)

Disk array:
- disk array ports (LUNs)
- logical unit (LU) options
- physical volume usage

Figure 3.10: administrator touch-points involved in creating a host volume for a file system or database.

Even a simple-looking operation entails many individual storage-component operations.

1. At the disk array, it is necessary to select a set of back-end disk drives, and group them together into a logical unit (LU) – after making appropriate choices about the RAID layout algorithm, the set of disks to pick (e.g., fast ones or slow ones, unused ones, or ones already partly full?), and properties of the resulting LU (e.g., should it have snapshots taken at regular intervals, or be mirrored remotely?). The disk array ports may need configuring – in some arrays, not all LUs are accessible to all ports, or should be (e.g., for protection). If the disk array permits, it may also be possible to impose host-specific access controls or throughput limits on the LU, or port, or both.

Automating
storage
management
will reduce
error rates,
reduce costs,
and increase
the storage
infrastructure's
ability to
respond rapidly
to business
needs.

2. An appropriate path through the storage network needs to be determined – typically at least two such paths are needed, to allow for failover.

3. If the storage network supports FibreChannel zones or Ethernet VLANs (virtual LANs, overlay networks for Ethernets), this security technique will need to be configured, making sure that switch, connectivity, or other limitations are not violated.

4. At the host, traffic to the new LU will need to be routed via at least two access ports (I/O cards) – perhaps with additional security configuration needed, or load-balancing or failover parameters established. For ease of later administration, the raw LUs offered by disk arrays are often fronted by a logical volume manager – a layer of virtualization to allow resizing, so this will need to be configured appropriately. Then, finally, the new logical volume is ready for its contents, which will doubtless come with a few configuration choices of their own.

Any one of these steps can go wrong – either because a resource is not available, or because some configuration limit is reached (e.g., the number of LUs that a network port can export), or because the administrator didn't type exactly the right thing (in one example setup we saw recently, mistyping a single digit – /dev/dsk/c47t1**5**d0 instead of /dev/dsk/c47t1**3**d0 – would have wiped out the Oracle database installation on that machine).

Each of the decisions made at this level typically results in some cost or consequence at a higher level (e.g., a mis-configured alternate network path for a mission-critical application might not be noticed until its primary path fails – and then there is no way to reach the data). Ideally, we would like to be able to tie decisions made at this level to those of the business organization they serve.

3.4 Automating storage management

Many studies have shown that human error is a significant component of failures in complex systems, and that people are not terribly good at repetitive, detail-oriented tasks. Moreover, the relative costs of people and hardware continue to diverge: a recent IDC study quoted storage-administrator salaries were on a par with the cost of the direct-attach storage they could manage in 2005, and within a factor of 2–3 for networked storage. With salaries increasing at 3–8% annually, and storage capacity costs dropping like a rock, this situation is only going to get worse.

Automating storage management is the answer. Just as in other fields of infrastructure management, taking human work out of the system reduces the likelihood of problems, speeds responses to issues, and reduces costs. In its advanced forms, automation enables greater business agility by allowing approved storage-infrastructure change requests to be satisfied in minutes rather than weeks.

As an example of the current state of the art, HP's Storage Essentials provides assistance with the more mundane parts of storage administration, by performing target-based discovery, monitoring, and reporting. It also offers basic control functions, presenting the data needed to do provisioning in a way that allows point-and-click selection of only the appropriate alternatives at each step along the way. But the emphasis is still on assisting manual processes, or on automating relatively straightforward responses to canned situations ("send email if less than 10% free space").

Plenty of opportunities to add value remain: in particular, in more automated configuration of the disk arrays themselves; and in automatically making smart decisions where tradeoffs are involved – such as determining which data should live on which kind of device. Expect to see more of this high-value automation over the next few years.

We will also see storage management become more tightly integrated with larger-scale datacenter management suites, and for it to become possible for automated *requests* to be made of the storage provisioning system, as well as automated responses being provided to human requests – this will allow a truly adaptive IT system, all the way up the stack to the business-management layer.

3.4.1 Policies, rules and goals

Automation is most effective when it can be driven by end goals, rather than simply eliminating repetitive tasks. (Unfortunately, some of the approaches to computer-based management do the opposite: as many system administrators will tell you, one reason they don't adopt graphical user interfaces is that point-and-click gets somewhat tedious after the first few hundred times: script-based interfaces offer considerably more power, at the expense of ease of use.)

Those end goals represent a way to capture the *intentions* of the user or administrator: capturing these would give us a better chance of automating the processes to achieve them.

One way to represent intent is by specifying (business) goals, rather than the decisions taken to achieve them. For example, "make it possible for an application to increase its storage space by 25% in a day or less", rather than "if the amount of free spaced falls below 2TB, then migrate 0.1TB of data older than 30 days to offline storage, unless we are within 2 days of the end of the month, in which case …". It is often simpler to define the end state than it is to enumerate all possible paths to achieving it.

The example in Figure 3.9 of automating the choice of data-replication technology did this: it used the business goal of minimizing the sum of outlays and penalties, and was neutral as to how those goals were achieved. This allowed the appropriate technology to be brought to bear in different situations.

Model-based automation is particularly well suited to this approach, because it separates the description of the current state (the model) from the reasoning required to decide what to do about it.

One popular alternative to the goal-oriented approach is to use rule-based policies, which are simply "*if <this condition is true> then <do this action>*" statements, or *rules*. This works fine for the first couple of rules, but gets bogged down as soon as the rules start to overlap. For example, if one rule says that marketing-campaign materials have to be moved to failure-tolerant storage, and another says that video files should be moved to cheap, unprotected storage, what will happen to a video advertisement for a marketing campaign?

One way to capture intent is by specifying goals, rather than the steps required to achieve them.

The unadorned term "policy" usually means a policy rule, although strictly it can also apply to a goal. *Policy engines* – software to manage and interpret rules – are useful tools, and often at the heart of automation systems. They are an intermediate step in translating business objectives down to storage management actions – but those objectives themselves are best expressed explicitly as higher-level (policy) goals, rather than as sets of lower-level (policy) rules.

3.4.2 Trusting automation

Unfortunately, the path to widespread adoption of automation is proving more difficult than anybody expected, and the industry is still struggling to achieve true simplicity-of-control. Customers are still slow to adopt technologies that require them to trust automated systems – they fear a loss of control, and that the system will make different decisions than a person might have made. Ultimately, the economic argument will make the transition unavoidable, so the real question here is how it could be accelerated.

One way to increase trust is to increase visibility into the automated actions the system is taking, and by repeated demonstration that the choices are appropriate. After a while, people will stop needing to look inside the box – in fact, they will find it tedious and unproductive to do so. When was the last time you asked to see the binary representation used by a spreadsheet, or the precise parameters used by the automatic transmission control in your car?

Challenges aside, storage management is an area where customers will be better served by more automation, and concomitantly less human intervention in the mundane, error-prone tasks involved.

3.5 Summary

Storage-infrastructure management is a rich field – one rife with opportunities for technical contributions that can have a significant impact on businesses – both storage customers and storage vendors. The key things to remember are:

- storage management encompasses many different tasks, applied to a bewildering diversity of storage devices and networks; it appears complicated because it is complicated;

- control and management of data replication functionality is an essential component in helping storage systems meet business needs; and

- automation is the key to controlling the complexity, but still has a long way to go before it is ready for widespread adoption.

4 Data/information infrastructure

One person's data is another person's information – and vice versa. The difference is context: context is what makes data meaningful, and turns it into information. A list of names and numbers is just raw data, until you know whether they are customer names and phone numbers, or a list of employee names and social-security numbers. Certainly, some information can be inferred: UK phone numbers typically start with a zero, USA numbers with a one or a 3-digit field and are 10 or 11 digits long, and USA social security numbers are 9 digits long. These implicit semantics are a kind of context, and help turn the raw data into useful information, although getting a computer to understand such rules is extremely difficult.

4.1.1 How much data is there?

Quite a lot – and the amount is growing rapidly. A UC Berkeley study[1] determined that approximately 5 Exabytes of data were generated worldwide in 2002, and the rate of data generation was growing at more than 30% per year. More than 90% of this data was stored on disk drives.

Although it is hard to quantify the amount of "information" that data contains, it does seem that the information-density of data is dropping as richer formats are more widely adopted. We used to be happy with plain text for email; now we use formatted documents like HTML, Microsoft Word, or Adobe's portable document format (PDF). They say much the same thing, but take more bytes to do so. Experience-rich, but information-poor, formats such as digitally-encoded music and video are becoming more prevalent, and further accelerating the trend.

---

[1] Peter Lyman and Hal R. Varian: *How much information*, 2003, http://www.sims.berkeley.edu/how-much-info-2003, accessed January 2008. Note: we use the term *data* to describe what this study calls *information*.

The scale of data [1]			
Kilobyte (KB)	1 000 (10³) bytes		
	2 KB: A typewritten page		
	100 KB: A low-resolution photo		
Megabyte (MB)	1 000 000 (10⁶) bytes		
	1 MB: A small novel or 3.5" floppy disk		
	2 MB: A high-resolution photo		
	5 MB: The complete works of Shakespeare		
	10 MB: A minute of hi-fi sound		
	100 MB: 1 meter of shelved books		
	500 MB: A CD-ROM		
Gigabyte (GB)	1 000 000 000 (10⁹) bytes		
	1 GB: A pickup truck filled with books		
	5 GB: A single DVD		
	20 GB: A good collection of Beethoven		
	100 GB: A library floor of academic journals		
	400 GB: An hour of raw (uncompressed) HD video		
Terabyte (TB)	1 000 000 000 000 (10¹²) bytes		
	1 TB: 500 000 trees made into paper and printed		
	2 TB: An academic research library		
	10 TB: The print collections of the USA Library of Congress		
	50 TB: A large mass storage system		
	200 TB: The largest relational databases		
Petabyte (PB)	1 000 000 000 000 000 (10¹⁵) bytes		
	1 PB: 100 days of raw HD video		
	2 PB: All USA academic research libraries		
	20 PB: Production of magnetic disk drives in 1995		
	200 PB: All printed material		
Exabyte (EB)	1 000 000 000 000 000 000 (10¹⁸) bytes		
	2 EB: Total volume of information generated in 1999		
	5 EB: All words ever spoken by humans		

The explosion is occurring largely because more and more information (or data) is being captured or created in digital format, thanks to the ready availability of digital sensors of all types. These include digital cameras (now becoming nearly ubiquitous in cell-phones), closed-circuit TV cameras, and point-of-sale terminals in shops and supermarkets, which gather enormous quantities of data about people's shopping habits.

Regulations are driving the retention of data for longer periods and for many purposes. For example, more data to analyze enables better fraud-detection and allows law-enforcement actions that help achieve a more transparent business environment for shareholders and investors. But increased data capture, storing, and retention is also being driven by the business benefits of doing so: data-mining over a month's worth (or even a year's worth) of purchasing decisions can improve

---

[1] Adapted from Peter Lyman and Hal R. Varian: *How much information*, ibid.

business decision-making by making seasonal variations more apparent, far outweighing the costs of storing the additional data.

And finally, data (and information) is getting ever more expensive to delete, because it often requires people's time to do it. And given the trends in the underlying storage technologies, what used to be expensive to store yesterday is much cheaper today – and will be cheaper still tomorrow. Although storing the data may not be a problem in itself, it may interfere with other, more important uses of the data. For example, too much old data slows down backups and searches; makes response times too long; and results in out-of-date information distracting from more recent, urgent results. In turn, this has led to the creation of software to help – for example, an HP product, the Reference Information Manager for Databases, offers technology to help offload no-longer-critical data from databases.

4.1.2 Structured and unstructured data

All data is structured. But the term *structured data* is reserved for information that the system (almost always a database) storing the data understands – everything else is (rather misleadingly) called "unstructured". "Unstructured data" includes application files such as presentations, spreadsheets, calendars, and address books. These are all perfectly well-structured objects from the point of view of the application that supports them, but their structure isn't understood by the file system and the storage infrastructure.

All data is structured, but some data is more structured than other data. A database of help-desk calls may contain a (well-structured) record for each call, but one of the fields might be "customer description of their problem". The structure of the data could be perfectly clear – a free-form text string, perhaps in the international-standard character set (Unicode), using the language of the call center (e.g., French), and having a maximum length of 1024 characters. But the meaning of each entry may only be readily accessible to a human. That is, the data is well-structured, but its information content takes work to extract.

4.1.3 Metadata

Even though a storage system layer may not understand what it is storing, it may still know a great deal of additional information about it. Such information is called *metadata* – which is simply information about data. (A commonly-used phrase is "data about data", but almost all metadata is both well-structured and exists in a known context.)

There are many types of metadata. Here are a few examples:

- *time:* when the container was created, last written to, or last read from

- *size:* how much data is there? (this can be measured in basic terms like bytes, or it might include things like the number of rows, or lines of text)

- *provenance:* where did this data come from? who wrote it? with what application? using what input data?

- *content-index:* pointers into the data for fast searching – indices have long been a mainstay of databases, and are becoming more prevalent for file systems with the advent of desktop and enterprise search engines

Metadata is simply information about data.

53

- *data type:* does the container hold text, music, video, a spreadsheet?
- *file- and folder-names:* the names assigned to data containers are themselves a kind of metadata
- *data quality:* whether the data is good, or should be taken with a grain of salt. "Good" could mean things like complete, correct, accurate, precise, internally consistent, consistent with external data, etcetera … or any combination of these
- *timeliness:* is the data up to date with respect to its source?
- *tainted:* was this data derived from a source that is suspect in some way (e.g., contaminated by a virus, or itself tainted)?

Some metadata is stored by the storage system (e.g., filename, access times); other metadata can be deduced from the contents of the data (e.g., size, record count). Some metadata is explicit (e.g., an index); other metadata is implied by other indicators (e.g., in a Windows system, a filename extension such as ".ppt" is usually a good guide to the file type, but it is only a convention, so may be incorrect).

An increasing amount of effort is expended by storage systems in deducing information about the structure and use of the data they store. This is occurring partly because the techniques for doing so have matured; partly because doing so is becoming of greater value as the amount of data increases; and partly because it is less and less cost-effective (or accurate) to have people provide such metadata manually.

Metadata management and use is important in many of the advanced information-management functions being developed today. There is a clear trend towards more aggressive creation, storing, and use of such metadata.

4.1.4 Storage systems provide containers for data

Storage systems provide containers for data (and thus information), at a number of different levels. We'll start our tour at the bottom of the stack:

- **Disk drives** provide fixed-size *block volumes* constructed from fixed-size blocks. The basic operations on volumes are *read-block* and *write-block*. Volumes are typically named and accessed via non human-friendly handles like /dev/dsk/c0d5t2.
- **Disk arrays** and **block-level virtualization** techniques aggregate and then "slice and dice" fixed-size block volumes into variable-sized ones – still with the same *read/write-block* interface, with the addition of *create-volume* and *delete-volume*.
- **File systems** pack variable-length vectors of bytes (called *files*) into block volumes. File systems also offer human-readable names, a folder or directory hierarchy, and operations like *create-file*, *delete-file*, and *rename-file*, as well as *read-bytes* and *write-bytes*. All modern file systems can handle millions of files in a file system; at least one can handle a billion files in a single folder. See section 4.2 on file systems for more details.

- **Databases** pack very regular data structures called *records* into *tables*, and then pack those tables into either volumes or files. Databases offer operations like *insert-record*, *select-record* and *create-table*. See section 4.3 on databases for more details.

- **Applications** use file systems and databases to store their information.

- **Repositories** store arbitrary data *objects* (such as files, or database records, or application data sets). They may use any combination of volumes, file systems or databases to store these objects, and offer operations such as *store-object*, *retrieve-object* and *delete-object*. See the later section on repositories for more information.

application

data:	application-specific content
container:	file (byte vector)

file system

data:	file (named)
container:	volume (virtual block vector)

volume-virtualization system

data:	volume fragment
container:	logical unit (LU)

disk array

data:	LU fragment
container:	disk drive

Figure 4.1: a sample content/container stack

One thing that might be confusing about this view of storage systems is that file systems appear both as a container-type (for files) and as the contents of another container (a block volume). The nit-picking answer is that the *representation of the files* in the file system is what fills the blocks in the block-volume, not the files themselves. But the simple answer is that it just works anyway – and, more importantly – helps describe what's going on by providing a simple pattern that can be applied in many places: *data (contents) is packed into storage (containers)*.

The remainder of this chapter concerns itself with the three most important systems that operate at the data-storage layer in the storage stack: file systems, databases, and content-repositories.

4.2 File systems

As noted above, a file system packs many variable-length files into a single block volume that is provided by the underlying storage system infrastructure.

Each file has certain well-defined metadata associated with it. The precise set varies a bit from system to system, but typically contains something similar to the following list, which is a summary of the specific metadata supported by the standard HP-UX file system:

Local file
systems read
and write to
locally-
available block
storage
volumes.

- *device (volume)* on which the file lives
- *inode number* – an internal identifier that makes the file unique within the file system
- *access control permissions* – can the file be read, written, or executed by the file's owner, the group they are part of, or everybody else? (An alternate form is an Access Control List, or ACL, which is a specific list of users and what each is allowed to do to the file.)
- *file owner* – the user account that "owns" the file (usually the file's creator)
- *file group* – which group the file belongs to (a group is a set of users whose access to the file can be controlled together – e.g., all the people in a department or on a project)
- *file size* – in bytes and the number of blocks it uses on disk
- *times* of last-access, last-write, and file creation

Each file has at least one *name*. Names are kept in *directories* (folders), and are usually implemented as a link to the target file. Keeping the metadata about the file itself separate from the name of the file makes it possible to give the same file multiple names.

The operations permitted on a file are relatively simple. You can create or delete it, rename it, read it, write to it (which can make it longer), truncate or shrink it, ask for the file's metadata, and change some of it (e.g., the owning account). Whether you will be permitted to do these operations is a function of the access control metadata maintained by the file system.

4.2.1 File system implementations

Local file systems are those that run on a host computer, and read and write to locally-available block volumes, whether those are provided by direct-attached storage (DAS) or SAN-attached block storage (e.g., a disk array on the other end of a FibreChannel fabric).

Each operating system type has its own family of file systems; most make it possible to use a different type of file system on different volumes. For example, on Microsoft Windows, the NT file system (NTFS) is the best current bet for almost all magnetic-disk-based uses. An MS-DOS era format is used for floppy disks (it's based on a simple data structure called a File Allocation Table (FAT), which gives it its name). CD-ROMs have their own file system layout, defined by an international standard. All can be supported on a single Windows XP system.

Similarly, Linux supports dozens of different kinds of file systems with different tradeoffs between ruggedness in the face of power failures, performance, and, in some cases, defect rates. The most commonly used are:

- *ext2,* which is relatively simple and fast, but unsafe in some circumstances,
- *ext3,* an update to ext2, which adds some safety and speed features,
- *reiserfs,* arguably the most full-featured, fastest and safest, and
- *xfs,* an open-source version of a file system that was originally developed by Silicon Graphics, optimized for large numbers of large files.

File systems have traditionally been an area for operating system vendors to compete against one another. Symantec/Veritas has established a strong foothold in this space, and offers a file system that runs on many UNIX variants.

The main technical differences between file system variants come from the design tradeoffs they make among performance, complexity, and ruggedness in the face of power and storage-device failures. The very simplest file systems read or write the storage device for every operation requested by their users. This results in poor performance, but is very simple to get right, requires a relatively small amount of software, and is resilient to many types of problem. It is used for things like floppy disks, flash memories in cameras, and storage devices that can be disconnected at any moment, such as a removable USB memory "dongle".

Much better performance can be achieved if the file system caches a copy of the most-often accessed data and metadata in a *buffer cache* in main memory. Instead of taking milliseconds to get the desired information from the block volume (e.g., disk), it can be looked up in microseconds from the main memory. But caching has a drawback: main memory is volatile, meaning that it loses its contents on a power failure, crash, or removal of the storage device. This is tolerable for data that has only been read – it can always be read again from disk.

Unfortunately, if a change is made to the cached copy and a power failure occurs before it gets pushed out to disk, the change will be lost. If the cached information that gets lost is part of the file system's own data structures, then it is possible that this will make the entire file system unusable, or at least wipe out a lot of user data. This problem is solved in practice by using one or more of the following techniques:

- **Don't wait too long** before writing out any changes to disk. This reduces the amount of data that could be lost. A typical value is 30 seconds.

- **Don't cache**: Microsoft Windows usually caches writes to its internal disks, but disables caching for removable media that can be disconnected at any moment, such as flash memory cards. The upside is that a user can unplug them as soon as they are done; the downside is lower performance.

- **Careful write-ordering**: make sure that any write to disk leaves the file system in a state such that any partly-finished operations can be undone – possibly with the loss of some user data, but without compromising the integrity of the file system as a whole. Typically, this means only writing recently-updated cached files to disk *after* the corresponding file system data structure has been updated (e.g., the list of blocks allocated to the file). Recovery after a crash consists of scanning all of the file system's data structures, looking for inconsistencies; if any are found, the ordering rules can be used to work out what was (probably) intended, and these fixes applied. This is the function of a "disk check" on Windows, or the *fsck* (file-system check) command on a UNIX system.

- **Journaling**: first, write a record to a log saying what the file system is about to do; then do it; then finally write a record to the log saying that it has been done. If something goes wrong, "replaying" the log will bring the file system back to a consistent state. This log replay consists of re-executing the parts of it that were recorded as going to happen, and undoing any actions that seem to have occurred, but weren't marked as finished.

The main differences between file system designs come from the tradeoffs they make among performance, complexity, and ruggedness.

A disk check can take minutes to hours; a log replay can often be completed in seconds. Hence, modern file systems tend to use journaling techniques. A second benefit that results is that appending to the log can often be faster than the one-at-a-time disk writes needed for the careful ordering approaches, so file system performance is also higher in the normal case, with no failures.

File system development continues: the current trend is towards more robust implementations and more widespread adoption of certain features:

- high-performance techniques such as journaling, and better access control techniques such as Access Control Lists (ACLs) – neither are particularly new, but they are still in the process of becoming ubiquitous;

- extended metadata support, e.g. for content-indexing and provenance;

- content-based naming, such as finding a file by running a search on its contents or metadata, rather than looking for its name;

- retention of past versions of files, allowing various forms of "time travel". This is useful for backup and error recovery.

4.2.2 File servers

A file server is nothing more than a computer system with a local file system that is made available ("exported") to other computers across a network. There are two common protocols for doing this:

- NFS (Network File System), which was originally developed by Sun Microsystems for Unix systems, but is now a well-documented Internet standard, with version 3 in widespread deployment, and version 4 being adopted by cutting-edge vendors and users.

- CIFS (Common Internet File System), which was initially developed by IBM, and extended by Microsoft for MS-DOS and Windows systems. Although the base file system protocol was submitted to an internet standards body in 1996, many of the extensions needed to make it useful in practice still remain proprietary. However, it has been reverse-engineered well enough for other vendors to offer CIFS-compliant file servers (so far as we can tell!). CIFS version 2 was released in 2007, with the Microsoft Vista operating system.

Both types of file systems are referred to as Network Attached Storage or NAS. It is possible to build a file server that supports both protocols, but some kludges are required to map the Windows and UNIX access-control models, locking and naming schemes onto one another.

On the client side, a specialized network file system (a kind of virtual file system, or VFS) takes the place of a local file system, and is used to access the remote file server on the client's behalf.

On the server side, file servers can be off-the-shelf computers, specialized, self-contained appliances, or a "NAS head", which front-ends an external block-storage system (usually via a SAN).

A file server is simply a computer that exports its local file systems onto a network.

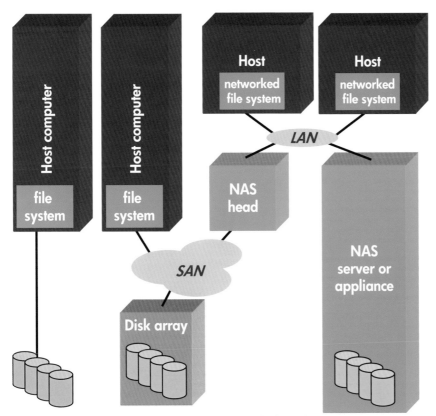

Figure 4.2: The SNIA Shared Storage Model for file-based storage systems

4.2.2.1 Why use specialized file servers?

Dedicated file servers (especially appliances, but to some extent NAS heads too) bring many advantages: they are often easier to manage than a general-purpose operating system that exports a file system; they can have specialized performance hooks (e.g., specially-tuned local file systems, buffer management, and network software); and they often offer functions (e.g., remote mirroring and special backup support) that are easier for the file server vendors to develop, deploy and support in a proprietary environment, than would be the case for an operating system vendor to do in the general case.

The disadvantage is a small cost premium if a computer system is already available to run the file service. Increasingly, the cost-of-management benefits are outweighing the hardware purchase cost, although software add-ons from the file system vendors are often eye-poppingly priced.

The most well-known storage appliance is the Network Appliances (NetApp) line, which has succeeded in part because it was founded on the business model of hiding much of the internal complexity of the storage stack from its administrators and users. (The fact that it used a proprietary file system to provide better-than-UNIX performance out of the box helped, too.)

4.2.2.2 Distributed file systems

One advantage of file servers is that they allow many client systems to access the same data. However, most file server protocols have some unpleasant behaviors (lost updates, or even file corruption) if more than one of those systems wants to share access to a single file at the same time. One way to fix this is to use one of the newer file server protocols, such as NFSv4 (Network File Service version 4). This can help to reduce problems, but may not eliminate them altogether.

Another technique is to have the client computers become peers of one another, and collaborate to run a *distributed file system*. Such file systems are very tricky to write, because they have to cope simultaneously with demanding performance goals, seamless integration with local file system behavior (the "holy grail" here is a so-called "single-system image", which looks and feels to all the applications running on the multitude of client nodes as if they were all running on the same local file system), and the multitude of failures that bedevil distributed systems.[1]

A huge amount of operating system research from the 1980s onwards has produced only a few examples of both technically and commercially successful distributed file systems – the Cluster File System shipped with Digital Equipment Corporation's VAXcluster (later renamed TruCluster) being the most notable. The research done was by no means wasted: it drove understanding of, and solutions for, the complexities of distributed systems of all sorts, and has influenced computer science for decades. Ultimately, distributed file systems fell out of favor, as they were all proprietary, and typically only worked with a single vendor's operating system. This may yet change if a single vendor manages to gain the upper hand with an implementation that can be deployed in many host operating systems.

4.2.2.3 File server virtualization

File servers (or, more correctly, file services) can be virtualized, just like other components of the storage stack. The most common purposes are:

- aggregation for greater total capacity or performance, and ease of management of a set of back-end file servers;
- load balancing across those back-end servers; and
- caching to eliminate some of the delays that can result across wide-area network links.

Building an in-band (i.e., in the data path), high-performance, virtualization engine for file system aggregation is quite hard: file servers already have quite high performance, so any virtualization engine has to be at least as scalable as the back-end file servers it is fronting.

---

[1] A famous quip on this topic is due to Leslie Lamport: "A distributed system is one in which the failure of a computer you didn't even know existed can render your own computer unusable." (from an email sent 28 May 1987).

60

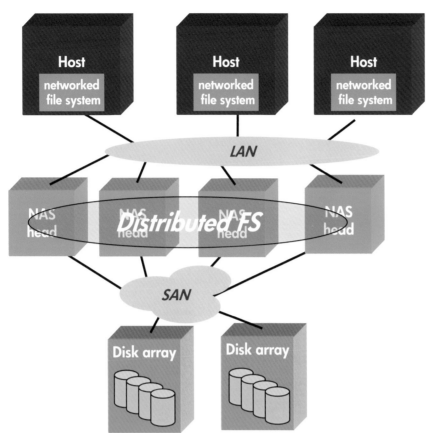

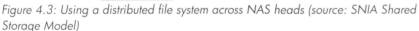

Figure 4.3: Using a distributed file system across NAS heads (source: SNIA Shared Storage Model)

As an alternative to a high-capacity file server, several companies and research efforts have focused on building file system clusters. Several architectures have been tried for building such systems, the most important being:

- *Partitioning:* Each file server system is made responsible for a specific part of the larger file system. If it receives a request for a different part, it simply forwards the request to the appropriate peer. This scheme is relatively simple to get right, but can have the effect of adding a network round-trip to many operations, and lead to performance "hot spots" if requests are not distributed evenly.

- *Shared storage:* Since multiple NAS heads can access a common back-end block storage device (e.g. disk array) they can build a single file system on that device, and all access it in parallel. Typically, some sort of distributed file system is needed to control who can access what, when. A good example of this kind of system is HP's Enterprise File Services Clustered Gateway. The scheme has the advantage that it can make use of existing block storage devices such as disk arrays (especially useful if you already have some, and wish to deploy file services), although having two tiers of storage system to manage is more complicated than just having one. Additionally, if not done carefully, this approach can result in scalability limitations.

Partitioning is relatively easy to get right, but can add network delay to requests. Shared storage file systems use a distributed front-end file system, leading to greater complexity, but potentially better performance.

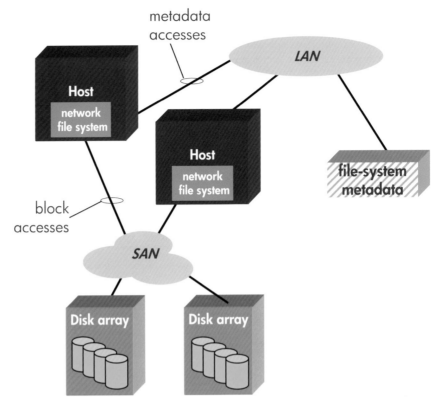

Figure 4.4: a file server implementation based on separating file system metadata from data (source: SNIA Shared Storage Model)

- *Out-of-band metadata:* A mid-way architectural point between file servers and a peer-to-peer distributed file systems is to use file-server like protocols for the complicated parts (basically file system metadata handling), and use direct disk access for the performance-critical parts (e.g., data read and write). Such systems are termed out-of-band file [metadata] systems, because the file-system metadata server is not on the critical access path between the client host and the target data. Since accessing the data is done directly by the client, these systems can be very fast and highly scalable. Deployment requires one of three approaches:

  - A new client-side file system for all supported operating system types, which is a lot of work (IBM's StorageTank and the Lustre file system take this approach).

  - Adopting a new file system protocol, such as pNFS (parallel NFS, an extension to NFSv4), that directly supports the separation of metadata and data.

  - Route non-participating clients via a dedicated file server interface that uses a backwards-compatible protocol, such as NFS or CIFS. This adds latency, but allows both old and new client file systems to be supported. Until pNFS becomes widespread, this approach is the one most likely to be successful.

Object-based storage devices (OSD)

While the out-of-band approach can be used with traditional SAN-connected block storage, it may be better yet with a storage device that is mid-way between a disk array and a file server: an Object-based Storage Device (OSD). An OSD is like a disk array in that it provides fast access to *objects* that are simply named using numbers (there are no folder hierarchies or nice names), and is like a file system in that the objects are variable-length, have local metadata (e.g., length, access time), and can be written to as if they were files. Panasas is a leading vendor in this field, which originated with a 1990s research program at Carnegie Mellon University. The first version of the OSD standard was adopted in 2004 as an industry standard by the committee responsible for the SCSI command set.

There is no "one perfect answer" to the question of how to build a scalable NAS service – each has advantages and disadvantages. The higher performance associated with the newer approaches tends to be accompanied by increased business and implementation risks – they simply have not had the same amount of testing as the older approaches.

4.3 Databases

A *database* is a set of structured data. A *database management system*, or DBMS, is an software system that implements such a database. A *database appliance* is a DBMS packaged in a set of hardware that runs a database as its only function. A *virtual database appliance* is a database appliance constructed using a set of dynamically-acquired resources, thereby avoiding the size- and performance constraints of dedicated hardware.

Almost all databases today are *relational databases*, which store data as records (or *rows*) in *tables*, and use operations in the relational calculus first described in 1970 by IBM's Edgar Dodd, and prototyped at IBM and UC Berkeley in the System R and Ingres projects respectively.

Essentially all relational DBMSs now use the programming language SQL (Structured Query Language) to access and configure their database. The two most important operations in SQL are *insert*, which puts rows into a table, and *select*, which runs a special search function to determine which rows to return. Performing an operation on a database is colloquially referred to as running a query.

The *select* operation can combine elements from rows held in different tables in a wide variety of ways, including complex conditional operations (e.g., "return an order record to me only if the supplier of the part it refers to is based in Texas"). The result is a rich, expressive language that is at the core of almost all commercial information processing today.

It is hard to underestimate the pervasiveness of databases: they are used everywhere from small data stores embedded inside applications (e.g., an address book for an email program), to the central underpinnings of enterprise-wide software such as supply-chain management. There are several reasons for this:

- the expressive power of the relational model makes it possible to build highly-functional data-processing systems with a few constructs;

Almost all databases today are relational databases.

- databases support *transactions* (see section 4.3.2) which operate as if each one was being run all by itself in the database, and make it much simpler to reason about the interactions that occur when handling thousands of customers simultaneously;

- transactions are also the basis for DBMS recovery – a transaction either completes (commits), or acts as if it had never been started (it aborts). This makes it much simpler to handle errors of many sorts, including power failures and system outages in the middle of multi-part operations.

All this has resulted in a multi-billion-dollar industry built around database systems. Space precludes more than a cursory mention of a couple of key technical points here.[1]

4.3.1 Databases in the storage-container stack

The following description is necessarily simplified, but it gives the general flavor. A relational database is organized as a set of tables, each of which contains rows. All rows in one table contain the same columns, which are named fields with a known type. Tables are thus the container for data rows.

The DBMS will typically collect together one or more tables (which are variable-sized objects) into one or more fixed-size table-spaces, which are the containers for tables; their fixed size makes the next level of space management simpler.

Table-spaces (or in some cases, tables themselves) are then packed into storage containers. Since databases are often performance-critical components, efficiency considerations used to mean that these storage containers were block volumes. However, the trend over the last several years has been to use files instead of block volumes. Files have a much more convenient naming scheme (a large database can need thousands of storage containers); are easy to grow or shrink; sit comfortably atop block-volume virtualization tools such as logical volume managers; and modern file systems provide essentially the same performance as the underlying block stores they are built on.

DBMS performance is determined by:

1. how well the queries can be optimized (reduced to their most efficient form);

2. how well the queries use main memory instead of having to go to disk;

3. how well the disk accesses that do occur are organized; and

4. how multiple concurrently-executing queries are choreographed and scheduled.

4.3.2 Transactions

In its most basic, commonly-used meaning, a *transaction* is just a set of operations on a database that run to completion as if there was nothing else going on at the same time – or, if that can't happen, that any changes made along the way are completely undone. In particular, transactions make it possible to do multiple

Rows of data in a database are packed into tables, which are then packed into block volumes or files.

---

[1] For more information, the reader is referred to Wikipedia, which has a good set of database-related articles at http://www.wikipedia.org.

operations as if they occurred all at one moment in time. (The standard example is that of transferring money from one bank account to another – either both the withdrawal and deposit operations should succeed, or neither. You also don't want a deposit to get lost because it is overwritten by a new value before the transaction has finished.)

By convention, the acronym ACID (Atomicity, Consistency, Isolation, and Durability) is used as a mnemonic for the desirable properties of transactions:

- *Atomicity* – all or nothing;

- *Consistency* – the database should be in an internally-consistent state at both the beginning and end of the transaction;

- *Isolation* – as if no other operations are occurring at the same time;

- *Durability* – the transaction won't get lost (e.g., due to a power failure) once the caller has been told the transaction has happened.

Much of the complexity in a DBMS comes from achieving all these properties simultaneously – while handling thousands of concurrent operations on terabytes of data, and in the face of potential system failures of many types.

4.3.3 Types of database

With such a wide range in goals – from simple embedded software managing a small set of tables for a cell phone's contact list, to huge enterprise data management systems that can run queries over a few years' worth of sale records – there are a range of different implementations, each aimed at a particular class of use. The most common classes are:

- **Embedded**: small, dedicated databases that aren't visible outside the applications they are part of. The market leader here is probably BerkeleyDB, developed by Sleepycat software and acquired by Oracle.

- **OLTP** (on-line transaction processing), used to process many hundreds or even thousands of concurrent requests, such as in the back end for online web services. The important measure here is the number of small transactions that can execute concurrently. Oracle and IBM's DB2 are the overall market leaders, with Microsoft's SQLServer a strong presence in Windows environments. Open source databases like MySQL are becoming increasingly common due to their much lower total cost of ownership.

- **Data warehouse/decision support/business intelligence**, used in forecasting and analysis operations. The important measure here is the time it takes to execute a number of large (long-running) transactions. Apart from the usual suspects (Oracle, DB2), NCR's Teradata has a strong presence in this space.

Rather like file systems, database software can be mapped onto its underlying physical computation infrastructure in a number of different ways:

- As software running on a single host. This is by far the bulk of the market today, with all the major vendors making their databases available in this form.

The major database types are embedded, OLTP, and decision support.

Repositories
specialize in
storing
information that
is near the end
of its lifecycle.

- Oracle also offers a scalable version of its database (Oracle 10g, where the g stands for "grid"), in which multiple smaller, and hence cheaper, hosts can run the database, and potentially replace a single large host.

- In the data warehousing/business intelligence part of the market, clustered database appliances are not uncommon. Because the performance bottleneck is often CPU and I/O bandwidth, rather than network traffic or memory, these approaches can bring the power of many individual database nodes to bear, run many queries at a time, and scan entire database tables in parallel. The current leader is Teradata, with Netezza and HP making recent entries.

Somewhat orthogonally to the above, database systems can also be distributed over the wide area – typically to achieve disaster tolerance. Because this requires replicating both data and computation capability, it is usually reserved for business-critical services. It can be accomplished by running on top of block-level remote mirroring services, or by the use of the log-based techniques: a list of the operations executed at the primary (or their effects) is copied over to the secondary and replayed there.

4.4 Repositories

Unlike file systems and databases, which support active data, *repositories* (or *archives*) specialize in storing information that is closer to the end of its lifecycle. Instead of just handling files or records, they typically store more general *objects* or *business records*. These can be almost anything: documents, emails, images, instant messages, files, or database records.

Compared to file systems and databases, repositories:

- Are typically more concerned with economical storage of large amounts of information, and about accurate application of record retention and expiration, than about access performance.

- Do not support in-place updates; instead, whole objects are stored and retrieved. The principal operations are *store-object*, *retrieve-object*, and *delete-object*.

- Experience write-intensive workloads. Such is the nature of business records: many are stored, but few are looked at again. Billions, if not trillions, of objects may be stored, a scale at which most file systems start falling apart.

- Retrieve content primarily by content- and metadata-attributes, rather than by name or file system path. Repositories are slower than file systems at navigating to information by path-like metadata, but they can handle navigation through richer and less homogeneous types of metadata.

- Share the indexing characteristics of databases. However, while database indices are typically optimized for answering complex questions posed against relatively uniformly-structured data, repository indices are optimized for answering simple questions against many objects, across a wide variety of object formats.

- Store much more metadata with their objects than do file systems with their files. For example, an X-ray image stored in a repository may have metadata attributes such as the serial number of the X-ray machine that produced it, the patient identifier, classifications and diagnoses added by one or more radiologists, privacy and retention indications, and provenance metadata indicating whether the X-ray image was transferred along with the patient from a different hospital.

- Handle a greater variety of metadata types than databases. Hundreds, if not thousands, of metadata *schemas* may be defined, covering a variety of objects. Adding or extending a schema is also much simpler, and a routine operation in repositories, with little or no administrative impact.

Due to the relative uniformity of their metadata structure, file systems and databases force applications to implicitly or explicitly retain large amounts of metadata about their stored objects in application-specific formats. By virtue of the relative richness and expressiveness of their metadata structures, repositories allow applications to expose significantly more of the metadata to the storage system. The term *application-aware storage* is often used when describing storage systems with embedded repositories.

4.4.1 Versioning, time-travel, and compression

Even though in-place update of objects is not supported in repositories, users are allowed to *check out* objects, update the metadata, and insert a new version of the object via a *check in* operation. Some repositories support *transactions* against metadata. All such operations result in new versions of objects being created over time. This is known as *explicit versioning*.

More advanced repositories are capable of *implicit versioning*. When objects are stored, these repositories locate similar objects already stored in the repository, and implicitly create an *edit list* of how the new object differs from the one most similar to it.

Since a large number of objects and versions may be stored, repositories use a variety of *single-instancing* techniques to reduce the amount of storage they need.

- In *whole object single-instancing*, an object with the same contents as an already-stored object will reuse the existing object's data, although the two copies may maintain independent metadata.

- In *sub-document single instancing* – also known as *delta compression* – parts of documents that are found to be in common are stored just once, yielding even greater economy of space, because both identical copies and near-copies can be compressed in this way.

Both single-instance techniques use hashing and fingerprinting of objects, wherein short, unique, digital markers are derived from the objects' contents, indexed, and therefore compared far more efficiently than the objects themselves could be.

Sophisticated repository implementations can show views of the repository *as of a point in time*. This is useful, for instance, in legal discovery where a question might arise as to what was known at the time a business decision was made.

Repositories also support role-specific views of information, which are more sophisticated than file system access controls, and more flexible than protection

Repositories use single-instancing techniques to reduce the amount of storage they need.

views offered by databases. These are used, for instance, to support compliance officers' needs and auditing requirements.

Advanced repository products support virtualization for information aggregation and capacity planning purposes, just like file systems and databases.

4.4.2 Repository products

EMC introduced its scalable Centera system in 1998. This is more of a platform for "fixed-content storage" than a fully functional repository: its main role is to store immutable (never-changed) content efficiently, and other functions have to be provided externally to the Centera product. An ecosystem has formed around Centera, which included Enterprise Content Management (ECM) vendors such as FileNet (acquired by IBM) and Stellent (acquired by Oracle). These products inevitably include their own repository functions on top of the content-store core provided by Centera.

After the acquisition of Persist technologies in 2003, HP released the Reference Information Storage Server (RISS) – a repository system with the ability to search both by metadata and by content. Later releases added single-instancing, versioning, and transactions against metadata, as well as a powerful framework for definition and extension of object metadata schema. RISS has recently been renamed the HP Integrated Archive Platform (IAP). The complementary Reference Information Manager (RIM) front-end makes IAP capable of ingesting anything from email communications, instant messages, and medical images, to files and database records.

4.4.3 Repository standards

The proliferation of repository and fixed-content storage products has led to a need for a standard interface to repositories and fixed-content storage. There are two main contenders: XAM and JSR 170.

SNIA is currently (mid-2007) finalizing an application programming interface (API) standard for fixed-content storage, called XAM, for "eXtensible Access Method". Numerous vendors are porting their products to use the XAM API, instead of the proprietary APIs offered by Centera and older versions of RISS.

The Java Community Process has standardized Java language interfaces for accessing information stored in repositories. The Java Content Repository (JCR) specification is defined by their JSR 170 and JSR 283 documents (JSR = Java Specification Request). Day Software is the leading proponent of these specifications and offers both JSR 170-compliant repositories and aggregation middleware. Open-source offerings, such as Magnolia Enterprise Content Management System (ECM) and the Jeceira content repository, also comply with these standards. FAST of Norway, a leading enterprise search technology vendor, supports searching JSR 170-compliant repositories.

4.5 Summary

There is no shortage of data to fill storage systems! That data is much more useful if adequate metadata about it can be built up and made available.

File systems and file servers are going to increase in importance in the coming years, as they acquire many of the performance properties that used to be associated solely with block storage devices, and continue to offer a more convenient interface than the rather rigid block-based volume systems.

Much of the world's structured data is stored in databases, for good reason.

Repositories are starting to play a larger role at the end of the information lifecycle. Their extensive search and metadata-management capabilities suggest that repositories will find new roles and uses that are only just being explored.

5 Management of information and data

Information touches all aspects of modern businesses – people, processes, and infrastructure. Whereas previous chapters have discussed the storage containers, and the management of those containers, this chapter focuses on the management of information and data that have been placed into those containers (e.g., documents in a file system or records in a database). In particular, it discusses the central role that Information Lifecycle Management (ILM) plays in such management.[1]

In its broadest sense, ILM is a term used to describe the technologies and processes used to manage information in digital format from cradle to grave. That is, ILM encompasses information generation, capture, or conversion from other media (e.g., by scanning printed documents); management of information in its digital forms; retention and disposition decisions; and the delivery of information to users through a wide variety of media and outlets, including electronically, via printing, and mobile devices. More narrowly, ILM is sometimes used to refer just to the processes that enforce data-retention policies and make decisions about which kind of storage to use for data. We focus this chapter on the intersection of the broader definition with the topic of this book – i.e., the management of digitally-stored information, and all that this implies.

---

[1] Many of the topics discussed in this chapter are as much about data as about information, but the ILM terminology is well established, so we adopt it here.

ILM is part of a larger ecosystem known as Enterprise Information Management (EIM), a term that refers to the comprehensive discovery, policy-based governance, and use of integrated information to add business value to an enterprise.

As a result, taking information's business value into account in information-management decisions, and achieving compliance with laws, regulations, and policies are both important aspects of ILM.

ILM adoption has been accelerated by a number of government regulations – most importantly the US Sarbanes-Oxley (SOX) act for business reporting and information management. HIPAA (the Health Insurance Portability and Accountability Act of 1996) demanded greater concern for privacy in healthcare information management, and the Food and Drug Administration imposed similar kinds of requirements on information management in the pharmaceutical industry. A recent revision of the FRCP (Federal Rules of Civil Procedure) has placed strong requirements on discovery, retention and disclosure of electronically stored information. In all cases, the regulations call for better document and records management; increased business process standardization, reporting, and risk management; and greater control over security and auditing processes.

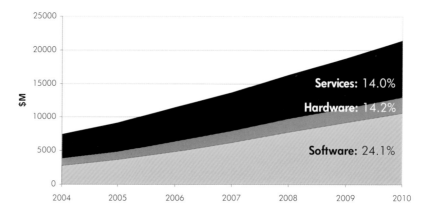

Figure 5.1: information-management revenue by year, with compound annual growth rate for 2005-2010 (source: IDC, Worldwide Compliance Infrastructure 2006–2010 Forecast: SOX 404 Requirements and the Emergence of the Records and Information Infrastructure Platform Define the Market, July 2006, IDC report #201961)

The result is that information management has turned from a small cost-saving exercise into a major compliance one. According to a survey in late 2005 of more than 325 companies,[1] more than two-thirds have automated compliance processes using information technology. Organizations were beginning to see results from instituting formal and automated information management, and enabling executives to maintain greater control over an enterprise's information assets. Fully three-fourths of the surveyed companies planned to reuse their compliance investments to

[1] Kevin Reilly, AMR Research Reports Compliance Spending Will Reach $27.3B in 2006, AMR Research, March 2006,
http://www.amrresearch.com/Content/View.asp?pmillid=19239

improve their business operations, with streamlined business processes (36%), better quality (28%), more secure information (14%), supply globalization (11%) and better visibility of operations (10%) listed as the main benefits.

Outside regulated industries such as finance and healthcare, most companies are facing additional privacy requirements for customer and employee information. Finally, as the knowledge worker becomes the dominant employee type[1] in one industry after another, productivity issues center more and more on information management.

All of these trends have generated considerable interest in – and demand for – information management technologies and processes.

5.1 The lifecycle of information

A convenient way to assemble and bring to bear a number of information management technologies is to organize them around the idea of an *information lifecycle.*

In the simplest lifecycle, information is created and then enters an *operational* state in which it is actively reviewed and modified. Typically, most information then enters a *transitional* phase, where it may need to be accessed occasionally. After some time, information moves to a *records management* phase, during which it is either deleted or moved to an archive or repository, from where it is typically very rarely accessed, if at all. (But if it *is* needed, it's probably *really* needed.)

Continuously protect	Optimize		Archive		
0 – 72 hrs	72 hrs – 2 wks	months	years		decades
operational	*transitional*		*records management*		

Figure 5.2: A simple view of a document lifecycle timeline

Some data needs to be archived for a very long time indeed – as much as several decades. This presents new technical challenges: the physical media used to store the original data, the data format, and even the application that understood it can all become obsolete (as discussed in section 3.2.3). A common first step is to convert the data from the application-specific form it had while it was being actively used into a format that is explicitly designed to be longer-lasting. For example, in 2005 the International Standards Organization (ISO) issued a standard for this purpose that used PDF/A, an archive-friendly form of Adobe's Portable Document Format, that includes font embedding and device-independent color-space management;[2] and HP's Database Archiving software uses a self-describing, XML-based format for data that it extracts from production databases when slimming them down. Subsequently, the data is periodically *refreshed* to keep its data format

---

[1] U.S. Bureau of Labor Statistics reports that knowledge workers make up 28% to 45% (depending on how you count) of U.S. workforce. http://www.bls.gov

[2] *PDF/A - The Basics*, PDF Tools AG, January 2007.
http://purl.oclc.org/NET/PDF-A-intro.pdf

and storage medium current, and *scrubbed* to ensure that it has not become corrupted in storage or in transit.

Consider the simplified information lifecycle scenario shown in the figure below.

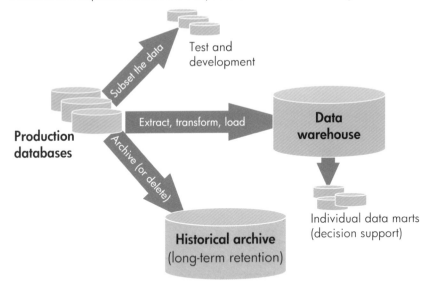

Figure 5.3: an idealized information flow from a set of production databases

A typical large enterprise has tens, if not hundreds, of operational data stores that support various business applications, ranging from supply chain management to point-of-sales transactions. There are numerous possible uses for the operational data that originates in each of these systems; the figure illustrates a few examples of reuse and transformation of this data:

1. Up-to-date data is frequently extracted, transformed, and loaded into a separate *data warehouse*, from which smaller *data-marts* are derived; both are used to support business-intelligence and decision-support operations.

2. Occasionally, a subset of the active data is copied, and used for application development and pre-production testing.

3. Periodically, or as needed, inactive data is extracted from the production systems and discarded, or archived for later reference, in a repository optimized for long-term storage.

There are many opportunities to control infrastructure and application costs via lifecycle actions on business records.

For example, consider the case of an online travel service. It might use a higher-performance, higher-availability database system to hold the records of passengers who have purchased tickets than for people who are "just looking". The information-lifecycle event that triggers the migration to the higher-quality storage would be a customer entering a credit card number. Data about frequent fliers' accounts would always be held in the high-performance system, to give them preferential treatment; and records of flights that departed more than 24 hours ago can be migrated to cheaper storage. Ideally, all this would be automated.

As a second example, consider a stock exchange receiving orders to buy or sell a security; orders that match become high-value transactions (trades) which make money for both exchanges and brokerages. Orders that never match still need to be retained but do not carry as high a business value. An exchange may maintain two classes of order books using different kinds of storage containers, where matching triggers the lifecycle action to migrate an order record from a low- to a high-value container. Again, ideally, all this would be automated.

Although compliance and cost savings are key drivers right now, ILM is also potentially a vehicle for business creativity.

5.2 The elements of ILM

Figure 5.4 illustrates the major sub-functions that make up the storage-related parts of the ILM process.

Discovery finds and identifies data – as well as learning which applications use it, and how they do so. It may also involve determining how to bring the data safely under the control of a migration system controlled by an ILM system.

Classification of data allows information to be placed into *labeled bins*, which become targets of policy statements. Classification often relies on metadata – such as tags – that describe the information content and context of documents and databases. Automatic classifiers can self-organize information into tidy clusters; trainable ones can learn from watching a human place labels on information.

Analysis extracts information from the data, and represents it either as a new information source, or as additional metadata. Analysis techniques cover a wide range; some look at extracting new features from a single document; others explore correlations and other relationships across hundreds of documents or sources.

Policy
frameworks are
a key part of
ILM systems.

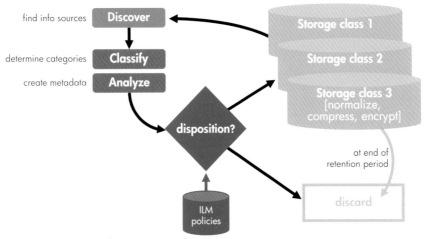

Figure 5.4: a view of ILM as a set of steps in a continuous process

Disposition is the process of determining what should be done with information. It relies heavily on **policy frameworks**, which are used to record and apply ILM policies for retention, deletion, and storage of discovered and classified information. They allow business intent to be stated declaratively; the ILM platform translates that intent into actionable decisions, and enforces them.

ILM policies are typically specified using rules (section 3.4.1), such as "encrypt all documents that contain customer-private information." Although they could also be declaratively specified using goals, such as "data in the mission-critical category shall experience no data-access outage lasting more than 5 seconds," there are few automated mechanisms for translating the latter into the former.

Normalization, or format-neutralization, is important for long-term retention of information, and allows it to be used by other applications than the one that created it. Normalization is typically applied when data is migrated into a repository. For example, when data in a proprietary, high-performance format is migrated out of an operational database, the ILM system can convert it to an open, text-based form, such as XML, as it is stored into the archive.

Managing redundancy: If the same piece of information (e.g., a document, a database, or a fragment of either) is copied and spread across many storage locations, the copies and versions will need managing. For example, redundant copies and versions may have to be suppressed for compliance reasons; doing so also reduces the amount of storage required.

Duplicate and near-duplicate documents (ones with minor changes in content or format) are surprisingly common: such redundancy accounts for 20–50% of information in enterprise documents; some users report as much as 70%.[1] Compression algorithms that exploit this can further reduce storage needs.

Some redundancy is essential if data is to survive failures (section 2.2), but too much is wasteful, and increases the risk of the copies getting out of sync. ILM systems can be used to drive towards the ideal: just enough copies being maintained to assure survival to a level commensurate with the data's importance. Extra copies of data without built-in redundancy, such as database records, can be made; superfluous copies of data that is inherently redundant, including many business documents, can be deleted.

Thanks to their ability to find and eliminate redundancy, the repositories used by ILM systems are capable of maintaining almost every version of every document ever produced in an enterprise (section 4.4.1). It is even possible to eliminate retransmitting data to a repository if it is already there, which saves bandwidth: important for wide-area links, such as between headquarters and branch offices.

Cost reduction can be achieved by migrating unimportant data to cheaper storage. ILM placement policies can manage this to good effect, ensuring that high-performance or high-availability storage is not wasted on low-valued data.

For example, data about out-of-date parts might be removed from an active-parts database stored on a mid-tier disk array, and migrated into an inactive-parts database, stored on a less expensive, lower-tier disk array.

Modern migration systems can go beyond policies based on file system metadata — such as document age, last-access-date, and file type — to ones that are application-, classification-, and content-aware. Their placement rules can also handle objects that need to move together, such as an email message and the files attached to it.

ILM systems are capable of maintaining almost every version of every document ever produced in an enterprise.

---

[1] http://www.forensics.com/html/whats_new_press_equivio.html

Compliance with prevailing laws about storage and management of information is a major driver of ILM adoption, as noted above. ILM platforms, such as the HP Integrated Archive Platform (IAP), offer compliance-oriented features not found in conventional storage systems. For instance, HP's IAP allows the creation of a compliance-officer's view into the shared repository that presents duplicated, time-stamped email communications of audited officers, and creates a searchable index of those emails. (This enables compliance with SEC 17a-4 – see the appendix to this chapter on page 84 for more information.)

Surveillance of stored and communicated information is a method of limiting business liability, by observing and detecting undesirable actions. ILM classification and analysis tools can facilitate such surveillance. If ILM processes can be executed in-band as information flows around the enterprise, it may even be possible to stop some actions before harm occurs. For example, corporate secrets could be prevented from accidentally being posted to a company web site; or inappropriate images could be blocked from being downloaded onto an employee laptop. Even without such enforcement, rapid detection and reporting will frequently help in mitigating the consequences of a problematic act.

Retention of data may be mandated for regulatory purposes. ILM can manage this by analyzing metadata, and adding (or using) classification tags that mark data with the appropriate retention period and policy (e.g., "delete within 1 month of the retention period expiring"). Retention may also be driven by the desire of a business to maintain a *corporate memory*.[1]

Deleting information reduces storage costs and supports business retention (deletion) policies: for example, the ISO 9001 standard requires that out-of-date product specifications be actively sought out and removed. Information may become obsolete because of its age or because of the existence of newer versions.

ILM processes
must be
executed by
systems whose
behavior is
both transparent
and auditable.

5.3 ILM processing requirements

Because ILM is so important in ensuring compliance, its processes must be executed by information systems whose behavior is both transparent and auditable. These systems often handle documents that may be used during legal proceedings, so certain aspects of their behaviors must be provable beyond reasonable doubt. Examples include: stored information hasn't been tampered with, searches are complete, and auditing is comprehensive.

Traditional storage systems cannot yet offer such assurances, so ILM processes are typically executed on specialized hardware/software platforms that can. The sooner that data is put into the ILM system, the sooner the requirements can be met. This means that capturing data close to its source, and rapidly migrating or copying it to a compliance-focused ILM platform, are likely to remain important parts of any near-term ILM deployment.

---

[1] A *corporate memory* is the total body of data, information and knowledge required to deliver the strategic aims and objectives of an organization. (Wikipedia)

5.4 The context of ILM

ILM is not a standalone process. The figure below shows some of the interactions between the ILM process steps discussed above and the external business processes and decision-makers around them.

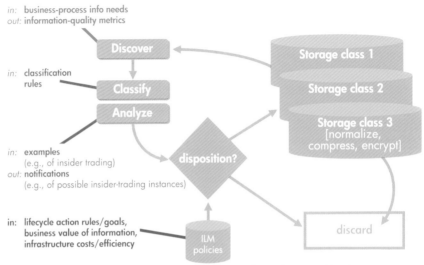

in: business-process info needs
out: information-quality metrics

in: classification rules

in: examples
(e.g., of insider trading)
out: notifications
(e.g., of possible insider-trading instances)

in: lifecycle action rules/goals,
business value of information,
infrastructure costs/efficiency

Discover

Classify

Analyze

disposition?

Storage class 1

Storage class 2

Storage class 3
[normalize, compress, encrypt]

discard

ILM policies

Figure 5.5: ILM processes must interact with people and external business processes to get inputs for the various processing and decision-making steps; in turn, the ILM system can inform those people and processes

Discovery is useful in ILM compliance solutions because it helps find and catalog information sources and containers, but its ability to find appropriate data sources is also valued in its own right. In some cases, discovery processes are able to provide quality-of-information metadata about those sources, too.

ILM systems use classification, analysis, and disposition processes to automate the handling of large amounts of information. They can also be used for other business purposes, such as detecting possible insider-trading events.

The disposition decisions that are at the heart of the ILM processes are driven by a set of policies and goals. These cannot come from within: they must be derived from the business context of the ILM system and the business processes that it supports (e.g., the business value of information, and how timely decisions must be). The policies may also take into account data from other IT systems, such as the relative running costs and capacities of different storage classes.

Because an ILM system automates application of these policies, and is capable of enforcing business goals, it is well positioned to support other business process innovations such as automation, optimization, and management of outsourcing.

5.4.1 Adjacent areas

ILM offers a good starting point for understanding and addressing the larger space of information management. The next figure outlines three broad areas that are adjacent to ILM.

ILM is well positioned to support business process innovation.

Figure 5.6: information management areas adjacent to ILM

5.4.1.1 Semantics

The first adjacent area is that associated with semantics, which is the *meaning carried by information*.

The more you understand about a piece of information, the better you can take advantage of it. For example, consider classification. If their contents are not understood, documents that appear similar will likely be placed in the same bin. Semantics allow finer-grained distinctions to be drawn, such as ones based on relationships among the documents (e.g., containment, composition, subordination). These can be used to create a network of meaning that can further partition the documents, or group them in helpful ways.

For example, consider a set of documents that describe how customs petitions should be handled. Some such documents might include the words "banana" and "mango" – words that have little to do with each other except that they both refer to fruits. That semantic knowledge would allow classifying all the documents about fruits together. It could also help to distinguish between similar-appearing terms such as "banana" and "banana republic."

In order for information semantics to be processed automatically, it must be described in a computer-readable language. In the last few years, advances have been made in such languages, which are used for describing, manipulating, and reasoning about the semantics of data.

These languages are used to express *ontologies* – formal conceptualizations of topics – which consist of some vocabulary of concepts and entities, their properties, and relationships amongst them. For example, if the topic is municipal bond trading, then the vocabulary might cover bond issuers, raters and ratings. Properties might include the state in which the issuer is located, and the relationships might define that Moody's (a rater) rates the debt issued by a certain city in New York as investment grade.

Semantics make it possible to specify (and act upon) relationships between different pieces of information.

Two common languages for ontologies are the Web Ontology Language (OWL) and the Darwin Information Typing Architecture (DITA). OWL was developed by a working group of the W3C (World Wide Web Consortium). DITA was developed by a cross industry working group; it originated as a language to aid the production and delivery of technical documentation.[1]

Both OWL and DITA are helping to expand the capabilities of information management systems to encompass the management and use of information in ways that exploit its meaning.

5.4.1.2 Business-process management

The second area adjacent to ILM is business-process management (BPM). ILM processes have many functions in common with other information management processes, especially around workflows for approval, audit, reporting and publishing. This suggests opportunities for reusing common elements of the infrastructure that support BPM and ILM.

Business processes often rely heavily on document workflows. The term *Enterprise Content Management (ECM)* has been used to describe the information management functions for such workflows, although more recent definitions suggest that it has largely become synonymous with the broader definition of ILM introduced above. As a result, ECM functions are being merged in with ILM implementations, leading to more uniform implementation of information-management policies, governing both the flow and the storage of information.

The discovery aspects of ILM can contribute to business processes by locating and providing access to the information sources needed by those business processes. To make this possible, business processes will need to inform the ILM system about the appropriate goals for the information they require, and the service level and content objectives they have for their information needs.

5.4.1.3 Information integration

The third area adjacent to ILM is information integration: merging information from disparate sources to create a useful, unified whole, even in the presence of differing concepts, contexts, and data formats. As noted above, legal pressures drive today's ILM systems to copy or move data onto the ILM platform. This means that they are effectively performing a kind of information integration using a centralized copy of the data. Once created, that centralized copy can be used as a resource for more extensive informant integration activities.

Modern integration technologies such as BEA Systems' AquaLogic suite support a decentralized approach to information integration: rather than requiring a copy on a centralized platform, they provide a single, consistent view of information that spans sources held at multiple sites. Modern policy-based governance platforms allow policies to be defined centrally but enforced in a distributed fashion by agents embedded within endpoints such as mail servers and file systems. It seems only natural to expect ILM to evolve in this direction as repository, ILM, and

Information integration merges disparate sources, even in the presence of differing concepts, contexts, and data formats.

---

[1] See http://xml.coverpages.org/dita.html for more information on DITA; http://www.w3.org/TR/owl-features/ for OWL.

compliance capabilities become more pervasive in external data containers such as file systems and databases.

This evolution will benefit businesses by allowing policy-based management of vast amounts of information, wherever it resides.

5.5 Trends in information management

The figure below illustrates a few areas where we predict overlaps between ILM and the three areas identified above will become more important in the near future.

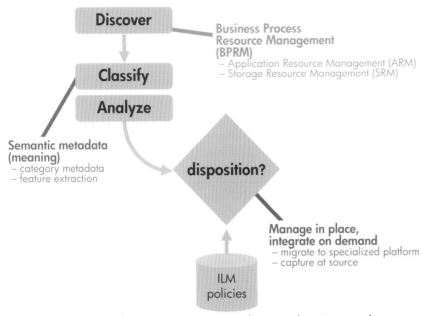

Figure 5.7: trends in information management, showing where ILM-specific functions are likely to co-evolve with functions from adjoining areas

Continued evolution of discovery. Discovery occurs at several levels of the storage stack. At the base level, discovery is about cataloging storage devices and their usage by file systems and databases. This is called Storage Resource Management (SRM), exemplified by HP's Storage Essentials product. The next level up is the usage of file and database resources by applications; this is the domain of Application Resource Management (ARM), and exemplified by HP's Reference Information Manager for Databases product, as well as by a plethora of file-level discovery products from Intermine, Kazeon and Scentric.

We believe that information discovery will continue to move up the stack, to the next level: Business Process [Information] Resource Management (BPRM), which deals with the use and reuse of information containers (file systems, databases and repositories) by business processes, and the requirements-driven discovery of the right information at the right cost in support of automation and optimization of business processes. One possible avenue for accelerating this trend is tighter linkage between ILM and ECM platforms.

Continued evolution of classification. The basic information-typing mechanisms available in an ILM system today are *definition* and *induction*. A typical definition is a policy rule that says "all data files updated by executables belonging to the payroll process should be in the *payroll* bin". A typical induction example is a program that learns to tell unsolicited email from good email by looking at examples of each. Induction is likely to become increasingly important.

Semantic understanding will extend classification by using knowledge deduced from the contents of documents. It, too, is likely to become more prevalent as ways of representing, capturing, and using that knowledge become better understood. Sophisticated commercial classifiers, for instance, are already starting to offer conceptual classification which goes beyond strict matching of search keywords, instead allowing a conceptual match between, say, the terms "football" and "sports."

The richness of the resulting classifications will increase pressure on rule-based policy systems, pushing them towards more automated rule-generation and testing.

Slow evolution away from specialized hardware platforms. Integration of ILM with in-place management of information and on-demand integration of information from distributed sources is a powerful concept. However, its realization is likely to be slow: most file systems and databases do not have repository-like features or any embedded ILM functions, and are not application-aware. This could take a few more years to reverse, although enterprise-strength distributed-policy-enforcement engines, such as Orchestria's IEC (Intelligent Electronic Control), are beginning to offer a scalable platform for centralized policy definition and a comprehensive set of agents for enforcing those policies in file systems, mail transfer agents, and mail servers.

Meanwhile, there continues to be a market for specialized, auditable, compliance-oriented ILM hardware platforms. These platforms have seen a growing ecosystem of hooks that let them bring data from diverse information sources onto the platform, where its lifecycle can be managed. An example of such an ecosystem is the one around HP's Information Archiving Platform (IAP), which includes email, file, and database archiving functions.

5.6 Summary

This chapter has briefly surveyed Information Lifecycle Management (ILM)-based techniques. Examining the connections between ILM and the broader information management area uncovered significant gaps and opportunities. ILM will continue to evolve from its current state, with its future adoption both spurred and limited by the ability of large vendors to fill these gaps and provide integrated solutions.

The following sums up our observations:

- Compliance, cost, customer privacy, information security, and the law are the principal drivers behind the adoption of ILM technologies today, especially in regulated industries. More businesses are embracing better ILM practices to protect their reputations.

Over time, ILM features will become more pervasive, and no longer be restricted to dedicated platforms.

- Once deployed, ILM systems create opportunities to locate and manage information assets by business value, enabling greater alignment between business and IT goals.

- Today's ILM component technologies – such as discovery, migration, and classification – will slowly evolve into embedded capabilities and integrated solutions that do not rely on a separate hardware platform.

- ILM platform vendors have an opportunity to sell software, solutions and services into adjacent areas of the information management market. Services-led engagements will enable broader adoption of information management.

5.7 Appendix: Regulations affecting information management

The following table[1] offers a concise summary of several of the regulations that impinge on information management. Some are applicable to a wide range of industries; some more narrowly focused. The variety and range suggest that society is paying – and will continue to pay – closer attention to the consequences of holding and using information.

Regulation	Key provisions
Gramm-Leach Bliley Act	Provisions to protect consumers' personal financial information as held by financial institutions.
HIPAA	Federal standards for transactions on electronic healthcare information, including security and privacy of health data.
SEC 17a-4	A 1997 amendment of laws dating back to 1934 allowed broker-dealers to protect investors from fraudulent or misleading claims in the securities industry, by storing records electronically. This includes records of electronic communications, such as email and instant messaging. Recent amendments accommodate immutable storage devices. Some compliance requirements: • Records preservation • Written and enforceable retention policies • Acceptable media (storage on indelible, non-rewriteable media) • Electronic storage availability • Record duplication and time-dating • Separate storage of duplicate records • Searchable index of all stored data • Audit systems and accountability
Sarbanes-Oxley (SOX)	This 2002 law changed financial practice and corporate governance by targeting accuracy and reliability of corporate disclosure and by mandating certification of financial reporting. SOX requires an audit control framework, beyond accounting, which must be acceptable to the accountants. Audit control includes the systems' infrastructure, and calls for a formal IT policy, security access controls. • Identify, capture and communicate information in an appropriate form and time framework • Be certain that the information is appropriate, timely, current, accurate and accessible

---

[1] Excerpted (with adaptations) from LeRoy Budnik, *Storage, ILM and Security Assessment, Planning and Design*, a course designed and offered by Knowledge Transfer, Inc. http://www.knowledgetransfer.net. Used with permission.

Regulation	Key provisions
FRCP	The US Federal Rules of Civil Procedure define processes and standards for conducting civil law cases in US Federal courts. The most recent update (2006) defined new procedures and expectations for the handling and discovery of digitally-stored documents and records.
ISO17799	Security best-practice reference, including sections on business continuity, development practices, compliance, and security for physical access, information access, and personnel.
DOE 10 CFR 600.153	This Department of Energy standard sets a basic retention period of 3 years for financial records with exception of anything under litigation. Nuclear plant records have *infinite* retention requirements.
DOD 5015.2	Sets design criteria for electronic records management software applications. Related to National Archives and Records Administration (NARA) regulations.
U.S. Patriot Act	Sets surveillance procedure and information sharing requirements. Direct impact on security and storage. It directs the hardening of infrastructure, and capture and retention of financial records and communications.
ITAR	International Trafficking in Arms Regulations place requirements on financial transactions processed by banks and other agencies. Failure to prove that the institution is in compliance may be taken to suggest that the institution is complicit in illegal activities.
FDA Title 21 CFR Part 11	The U.S. Food and Drug Administration provides guidance, under financial penalties for non-compliance, for the maintenance of electronic records. It is particularly stringent with regard to the pharmaceutical industry. Requirements include audit, chain of custody, copy management and record retention along with digital signatures. Unique provisions govern development entities from one or more parent companies. On assimilation of the child or if the child closes down for any reason, the parent company must acquire all required data, tests and samples. The chain of custody must remain unbroken. Requirements are strictly enforced.

Regulation	Key provisions
HSISA	The U.S. Homeland Security Act regulates information sharing and sets minimum requirements within the intelligence community for its interactions with other government organizations. Some of these requirements cover: • data integrity through the timely removal and destruction of obsolete or erroneous information • security and confidentiality of information • efficient and effective sharing of information • transmitting unclassified or classified information • restricting delivery of information to groups specified by geographic location, type of organization, position of a recipient within an organization, or a recipient's need to know
California SB1386	This law requires any state agency, person or business that conducts business in California, to disclose any security breaches of their personal information to California residents. The only reason for delay in notification is if law enforcement determines that notification will impede a criminal investigation. The importance of this legislation is that other countries, states and municipalities are using this law as a template for their own legislation.
New York Reg. 169, 173	These regulations in the State of New York discuss privacy of non-public health and financial records. They detail the responsibilities of state license holders in the insurance industry. They require a comprehensive, written security program for the protection of customer information that applies to companies as well as independent agents and adjustors.
E.U. Data Protection Directive of 1995	This legislation is the starting point for an evolving set of laws, updated at approximately two-year intervals. It covers a broad scope from the processing of data through the telecommunications sector to privacy issues on the Internet. In particular, it requires appropriate security in electronic communications and the maintenance of communications confidentiality. It has particular sensitivities to traffic analysis because telephone records were used during World War II to trace people. The most recent policy became effective in 2003.
Basel II	The Bank of International Settlements sets policy for international monetary and financial transactions – it is the central bank of central banks. Basel II covers all aspects of banking; of particular interest here are systems audit and security requirements, which go well beyond maintaining authentication records and transactional integrity. Any financial entity that does business outside its home country may find itself subject to some aspect of Basel II.

Regulation	Key provisions
PIPEDA	The Personal Protection and Electronic Documents Act (PIPEDA) is a comprehensive extension of existing Canadian law to "support and promote electronic commerce by protecting personal information that is collected, used or disclosed in certain circumstances." The law outlines strong protection requirements for personal information, including putting restrictions on government release without the consent of the individual to whom it relates. As in European legislation, it asserts that the individual should have some control over information stored about him or her.
Australian Commonwealth Privacy Act	The National Privacy Principles outlined here cover collection of personal information, its use and disclosure, data quality, data security, openness of personal information management policies, making identifiers anonymous, and restrictions on trans-border data flow.

6 Summary

We have come to the end of our overview of storage systems technology, and the data/information management systems that are layered above it. Our goal was to make this material more accessible and to communicate why users of the technology make the decisions they do. By way of a short summary, here are a few key messages and trends from each of the four areas we covered.

6.1 Storage infrastructure

Modern storage systems are built on the foundation of magnetic disk drives – which are both spectacular pieces of engineering, and possessed of access characteristics that much of the storage software stack spends a great deal of effort working around.

Block-based disk arrays provide highly reliable storage, and are the dominant storage components in data centers today. Redundancy is the key to this.

Storage networking allows storage and its clients to be separated, which in turn allows for storage resources to be pooled for economies of scale and ease of management. Several different storage network types exist, and although the move to IP based storage networks is inevitable, its pace is still a matter of debate.

Finally, magnetic tape remains an important part of the story, although most innovation and growth occur in the disk domain.

6.2 Storage infrastructure management

There are many challenges faced by a system administrator trying to manage a large and heterogeneous storage infrastructure and the sophisticated software components in it. Storage infrastructure management appears complicated because it is complicated.

People represent a significant – and growing – fraction of the cost of managing a storage system, both directly and because they are responsible for introducing many errors. The hope is that increased use of virtualization and automation will alleviate this. Although this has proven technically difficult, we expect that there will be major advances in this area in the coming years.

A trend in storage infrastructure monitoring and reporting functions is to separate the low-level information-gathering from higher-level analysis and decision-making functions. The increasing adoption of the SNIA Storage Management Initiative Specification (SMI-S) is helping to make this possible. In turn, increasing support for, and use of, model-based automation will make it possible to extend the number and reach of the value-added functions built above a broadly-deployed data-gathering layer.

Datacenter management software suites (e.g., HP's Systems Insight Manager) will eventually take on a larger share of the storage-infrastructure management. They will go beyond simply integrating the various user interfaces and advance to truly integrating the execution of the storage and information-related tasks. Increasingly, integrated control functions will take these suites beyond mere monitoring and reporting.

6.3 Data/information infrastructure

There is a lot of data in the world – and the quantity is increasing rapidly as digital data capture devices become more prevalent. The three most important tools used for packing data into storage systems are file systems, database systems, and content repositories.

Obtaining, creating, and using rich metadata – information about the data – is the key to extracting additional value from that data, and this trend will continue.

File system development continues, with the current trends being toward more robust implementations and more widespread support for metadata- and content-based access methods, such as query and search. Thanks to their greater ease of use, and increased performance, file servers will continue to become more important as the primary interface to the underlying storage system.

Databases have been, and will continue to be, key for structured information management.

The relatively new fixed-content repository systems, designed for storing large quantities of information near the end of its lifecycle, will become more important, thanks to continuing regulatory and compliance pressures.

6.4 Data/information management

Compliance pressures are resulting in a more formal set of approaches to the management of information over its lifetime, and the development of suites of Information Lifecycle Management (ILM) tools. These suites will enable businesses to tighten the linkages between the business value of their information and the policies governing its storage and management.

6.5 Conclusion

Massive amounts of digital information are with us today, and more is being collected, at an ever-increasing rate. But this – and the technology we describe – is not the end goal: what matters is how we make good use of information and the technology around it to make better-informed decisions that improve our businesses and our lives. We hope this book makes a small contribution towards furthering this goal.

Index